# THE SALMON COOKBOOK

# THE SALMON COOKBOOK

*Tessa Hayward*

*A Jill Norman Book*

*EBURY PRESS*
Published in association with
The Shetland Salmon Farmers' Association

First published 1992 by Ebury Press
an imprint of the Random Century Group
Random Century House
20 Vauxhall Bridge Road
London SW1V 2SA

British Library Cataloguing in Publication Data

ISBN 0 09 177027 0

Designed by Behram Kapadia
Back jacket photograph by Martin Norris

Filmset in Goudy Old Style by SX Composing Ltd, Rayleigh, Essex
Printed and bound in Singapore.

# CONTENTS

*For JDRH – with love*

# Acknowledgements

In writing this book I have had much help and encouragement and would like to thank, firstly, all those whom I have named in the text. In addition I owe particular gratitude to the following: Pat Hardcastle, Julian Cotterell, Michael Schneideman, Annabel Stapleton, Ann Minoprio, Julia Lyster, Mary Janson, Erica Harman, Gisella Clanmorris, and the many friends who have come and tasted and eaten and pronounced. I am also indebted to Jill Norman for her patience and help and her ability to get to the heart of a manuscript.

But this book would not have happened had it not been for Clive Hardcastle, whose idea it was, and for Gilean Mackenzie-Welter. I would add especial thanks to all those in Shetland who were so kind and helpful when I was up there: Michael Peterson, Frances Slater, Anne-Lise Smith and Debbie Hammond; and to James Moncrieff and the Shetland Salmon Farmers' Association. I, and a very fat and satisfied black cat, are most grateful to each and every one of them.

# INTRODUCTION

For many good reasons the salmon has long been regarded as the King of Fish. Its beauty is majestic; its life cycle extraordinary; the sight of a lithe and glistening fish leaping up-river is a spectacle never to be forgotten; and the thrill of excitement an angler experiences on landing a salmon is unique. If a fish can be romantic, this is it.

To be more practical, the salmon makes marvellous eating. The beautiful pink flesh with its fine texture and taste is undoubtedly one of the most versatile foods we have. Now, thanks to farming, salmon has become available in abundance and at affordable prices and eating it need no longer be restricted to special occasions. A rarity no more, it remains a great treat. It is a newly liberated food, and as such, should be experimented with and enjoyed to its full potential.

I have tried in this book to cover all aspects of salmon cookery, but I make no claim to its being comprehensive or complete: that would be impossible. I hope you find my ideas both useful and instructive, that the recipes set your taste buds going and that you have both fun and success when cooking them.

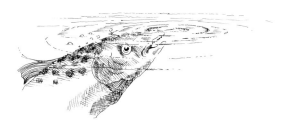

The recipes, unless otherwise stated, are all for four people.
Throughout the book, the eggs used are size 2.

# SHETLAND AND SALMON FARMING

## *Shetland: the place*

The remote and beautiful Shetland Isles lie some 100 miles offshore, almost equidistant from Aberdeen in Scotland, Bergen in Norway and Torshaven in Faroe. There are around 100 islands, 15 of which are inhabited. Nowhere on Shetland is more than three miles from the sea and there are, round every corner, breathtaking views of the land, the sea and the voes, as the inlets or lochs are called.

Shetland, as a glance at the map will show, is on the same latitude as St Petersburg, but thanks to the Gulf Stream, which swirls over the shallow continental shelf to the west of the islands, it does not suffer from the same extremes of temperature. Its climate is temperate; it has a low rainfall, mild winters and pleasant summers, with lots of sunshine and long days; there is a period in mid-June, known as the Simmer Dim, when it remains light all round the clock.

The Shetland landscape is bare, the winter winds that sweep the islands are not conducive to the growth of trees or high vegetation, and the heather-covered hills are made up mainly of peat, which is still traditionally cut and used as fuel. Sheep graze everywhere and their wool is used for one of the great and original industries of the islands: the production of Shetland sweaters. The Fair Isle designs are thought by some to have evolved from garments worn by Spanish Armada sailors who were shipwrecked on Fair Isle in 1588; whatever its origins, the tradition carries on and children in primary schools are still taught how to knit the intricate patterns.

Shetland is one of the great nature reserves of the British Isles and the bird observatory on Fair Isle has recorded more species than any other locality in Britain. At some times of the year the cliffs are crowded with nesting and noisy birds, and everybody, from the amateur to the ornithologist, can enjoy watching and listening.

The attractive and amusing puffin, with its triangular marked eyes and distinctive colouring, has almost been adopted as the symbol of Shetland and its picture appears on most postcards and pieces of tourist literature. The puffin spends the winter months flying endlessly in search of shoals of the tiny sea fish on which it feeds, and lives on the land only during the summer breeding period, when it can be seen scuttling in and out of its nest in dark burrows or crevices along the cliffs.

Other nesting birds include gannets – it is fun to watch them plunging dramatically from the cliff tops to pick fish from the sea; guillemots and shags. There was great excitement when in 1967 snowy owls were found breeding on the island of Fetlar, as it was the first time they had been recorded doing so in the British Isles. They stayed, hatching and raising their young for nine years, before returning to their more usual arctic haunts.

Little shaggy Shetland ponies are seen grazing on the pastureland. In the early years of this century many of them were sent to Scotland and England as their small size made them especially suitable for use as working ponies in the coal mines. Now their days as workhorses are over and they are kept for fun or to train as children's ponies.

The surrounding sea harbours fish of all kinds and their swimming predators, which include dolphins, porpoises and pilot whales, can often be spotted. Common and grey seals are a familiar sight on the shoreline and breed on many of the more isolated stretches of coast. Their population has been on the increase over the last few years. The otter, now happily protected, is another favourite and very attractive animal and near Sullom Voe, where many of them breed, the islanders have put up road signs with the warning 'Beware Otters Crossing'.

The richness of the wildlife is one of the heritages of the islands, and both the Royal Society for the Protection of Birds and The Nature Conservancy Council are well aware of the need to preserve it. When the Sullom Voe oil terminal was built environmentalists and conservationists worked alongside the oil companies to try to ensure that the enormous amounts of oil that would flow through the pipelines would do no damage to either the countryside or the wildlife. Everything is carefully and constantly monitored with the tankers having to observe very strict regulations. As a result there have been few problems, and wildlife and industry are living happily together.

## Shetland: the story

The Shetland Islands may be remote and isolated, but they have a rich and long history with archaeological evidence of occupation as early as the Stone and Bronze Ages.

Jarlshof, a settlement at Sumburgh on the southern point of mainland Shetland, was given its name by Sir Walter Scott and is one of the most complex and fascinating archaeological sites in northern Europe. It is neolithic, dating from around 1000BC and research has revealed 3,000 years of continuous occupation. Built of stone on the edge of the sea, it consists of many separate, mainly round structures, each covered with a peat roof. The unique defensive stone towers known as brochs were built in about 500BC, during the iron age. The ruins of several of these brochs can be visited and that at Clickimin on the edge of Lerwick looks especially dramatic under floodlight.

After the dark ages, the Norsemen arrived, and Shetland's prosperity really took off. At the end of the Viking Age, around 1000AD, the Norse population is thought to have been 22,000, which is slightly lower than today's. Shetland was ruled by Norway until the disasters of the Hanseatic League and the Black Death meant that it, along with Norway, was absorbed by Denmark. In 1469, King Christian of Denmark mortgaged Shetland to Scotland in lieu of a dowry for his daughter; she died before her marriage but Shetland remained in Scottish hands. The islands were then dominated by the unpopular and iron-fisted Scottish lairds, but the unification of Scotland and England in 1707 meant that Shetland became part of Britain and the influence and power of the remaining lairds steadily diminished as they returned to their native Scotland.

Throughout all these changes a Shetlander remained a Shetlander, proud of his Viking background but also acknowledging the stimulating influence of new blood from shipwrecked sailors and visiting fishermen. Certainly a degree of Spanish blood came from the ship that foundered off Fair Isle after the Armada in 1588, and sailors from French, Dutch and other European ships were also, from time to time, stranded on the islands. Shetlanders developed a language of their own, which is a mixture of English, Norse and Scottish; islanders still speak the dialect among themselves.

For many years the islanders lived off fishing and, to a smaller extent, wool. The heyday of the herring fishery industry at the end of the last century led to great economic prosperity and a rise in the population to over 40,000. The First World War seriously disrupted the community, leaving a period of considerable economic instability, poverty and emigration. The fishing industry was in disarray, there were hardly any boats left and little or no capital to build new ones. Fishing was just picking up again when the Second World War intervened. This, too, was followed by a period of hardship, which led to more people leaving the islands, especially for New Zealand and, to a lesser extent, Australia. Nowadays, many of the young Shetlanders save up and spend a year or so travelling to visit friends and relations in the Antipodes.

The mid-1960s and early 1970s were the great turning point for Shetland's economy. Fishing was again profitable, and then oil was found. Life on Shetland would never be the same again. Under British law, mineral rights belong, not to the individual, but to the state, so Shetlanders did not own their liquid gold and could only watch while the new enterprise was established.

Shetland has, in fact, benefited greatly from the oil in prosperity and employment, but this has not been allowed to disrupt the everyday life of the level-headed islanders. The industry has remained an entity on its own with the rigs well out to sea and the terminal at Summon Voe tucked away at the northern end of Mainland Shetland, but there are now some good modern roads and, at Sumburgh, an up-to-date airport with frequent flights to mainland Scotland.

The Shetland Council sees that money generated by the oil boom is carefully and wisely spent to ensure the future of Shetland and its people. In their interest, the Council helped with the modernization of the fishing fleet and supported the infant industry of salmon farming.

## Farming: the beginning

The Norwegians pioneered salmon farming in the early 1970s, and the Scots soon followed them. By the end of the decade an important new industry had been established, and during the next ten years it was to boom, with production almost doubling every year. However, supply caught up with demand, and the number of farms and the amount of fish produced has stabilized. Recent years have seen more call for quality fish reared with maximum care and minimal use of chemicals.

Shetlanders carefully watched Scottish salmon farming from the beginning, but they had a problem in setting up their own salmon farms. Young salmon, or smolts need to live for the first year in running fresh water, but there are no rivers in Shetland, because the rain either soaks into the peat in the bare countryside, or runs directly off the land into the sea. This meant that there was limited scope for hatcheries like those being established along estuaries on the west coast of Scotland, and that Shetland would have to import the bulk of its smolts ready for transfer from fresh to sea water. Transport was the next difficulty and this was finally overcome when the Norwegians developed a boat with tanks that had constantly flushing sea water. Now live smolts could be transported from the Scottish hatcheries and salmon could be farmed in Shetland.

The first farms were established in 1982, and Shetland has proved itself to be an almost perfect place to grow salmon: there is no land to the west for many hundreds of miles, and the crystal clear North Atlantic sweeps in and out of the cages which are anchored in the voes. The climate is mild, the average mean air temperature varies only by 8°C/15°F throughout the year (4-12°C/30-54°F), the islands seldom have long periods of frost or heat and the sea temperature remains constant and cool. The long northern summer days also contribute by giving the fish a good growing period.

To begin with the farmers went to Norway to learn the technology and husbandry and the very first salmon were sold through outlets there, but when the farms increased in number and size, the Shetland Salmon Farmers' Association was born. With fish now being produced in quantity, local sales companies were established, and Shetland salmon became widely available in Britain.

Thanks to modern technology, and the ability to recycle fresh water, the Shetland farmers now buy 25 per cent of their smolts from hatcheries established in their own islands, and salmon farming has become a truly local industry.

## Rearing the salmon

A hen salmon produces thousands of eggs in a season, and in the wild, only a handful of these will hatch and grow to reach maturity. However, farming dramatically reduces natural wastage and means that relatively few fish are needed to produce the stock required. The eggs are fertilized and placed in hatching trays. Minute alevin, as they are called, soon hatch out, and after about six months have developed into recognizable small fish known as fry.

The fry are transferred to much larger fresh water tanks where they reach the next stage in their growth and at about 5cm/2 inches long, become parr. The parr remain in the tanks for about a year, when their name is changed yet again, and they are known as smolts. A smolt is around 15cm/6 inches long, has achieved the colour and shape of a salmon, and is ready for transfer from fresh to sea water.

It is at this stage that the farmer takes over. He buys the smolts and transfers them to his farm, which consists of large fish cages anchored in the sheltered sea inlets around Shetland. Great care is taken when transporting the fish from the hatcheries to avoid them being injured or coming under any stress. The smolts are sometimes taken out to the cages in a special oxygentated container that is suspended under a helicpter and lowered gently into the sea.

The salmon live in sea water until harvesting and it is the farmer's job to care for them, and to produce the superior quality fish for which Shetland is famous.

## Growing salmon

Shetland is small, and although it seems impossible to drive for more than a minute or two without seeing the sea or a voe, the existing 65 farms use up nearly all the sites available.

The salmon cages are rather like vast shrimping nets; they vary in size and shape but they usually comprise floating round or square structures with nets up to 15 metres deep suspended from them. In order to facilitate the feeding and inspection of the fish, several cages are often joined together with walkways around and between them.

Adequate swimming space is considered essential and, to avoid overcrowding, the fish are moved into other cages as they grow: they always have considerably more space than is laid down by EEC directives. This, combined with the strong tidal flow, gives the right conditions for the production of well exercised and healthy fish.

The fish are fed three times a day, then, when they are bigger, twice. One or two farmers use very sophisticated computerized mechanical feeding systems, but many prefer to hand feed, saying that it keeps them in constant touch with the fish and enables them to spot a problem almost before it exists. The farmer seldom misses more than a day a year, making the boat journey to the cages to feed the fish even when the terrible winter gales sweep round the islands.

The feed is a special fish meal derived from the kind of species salmon would eat in the wild, and containing all the minerals and vitamins needed for healthy growth. The salmon are also fed small quantities of a natural substance, astaxanthin. This pigment is found naturally in wild salmon, whose diet includes prawns and shrimps, and gives the fish its characteristic pink colour. (It is interesting to note that the flesh of Baltic salmon, which do not feed on shellfish, is white.)

The fish grow quickly and after a year will have reached 1-2kg/2¼ – 4½lb. They are grown on for a few months and are normally killed humanely after 18 -24 months in the cages. The average weight of the fish when harvested is 3.5kg/7½lb, but quite a few will weigh 7 – 8kg/15 – 17lb. Every year the farmers have a competition for the biggest fish produced, and some real whoppers are entered, with the winner weighing somewhere over 14kg/30lb. The farmers would be the first to tell you that no fish would reach that size unless it had been given lots of tender loving care.

Watching the fish in the cages, jumping for food or a wayward fly, flashing silver in the sunlight and then disappearing, quietly and powerfully, into the depths, is impressive. The salmon seem alert, happy and in no mood to give up their title of 'king'.

## Grading and packing

After harvesting, the fish is immediately chilled for transport to one of seven packing stations. Within a few hours the fish are graded, weighed, and packed with a quantity of ice in insulated polystyrene boxes. The quality mark labelling a fish as 'superior' is given only to a perfect specimen. Fresh superior salmon have a Shetland tail tag which gives a best before date with instructions that the fish should be stored at below 2°C/36°F.

Every box of superior fish is individually labelled. The label indicates the number of fish in the box and the overall weight. The box also has a special Shetland Seafood Quality Control superior fish sticker, which is bar coded with an individual number. The computer holds all details of date, farm, packing station, and size of fish, and should there be any complaint, every box and every fish can be traced immediately.

## Quality control

All the farmers are represented by the Shetland Salmon Farmers' Association, which oversees every aspect of the industry. It helps iron out any problems they may have, and is committed to the production of high quality farmed salmon that is both safe and healthy for consumers and environment alike. Jimmy Moncrieff of the SSFA says: 'If you can't be the biggest, you have to be the best,' and: 'If you can't compete on volume, prosper on a premium.'

Another body, Shetland Seafood Quality Control (SSQC) was formed in 1985 and is a quality control company for all Shetland seafood. The company is independent; 50 per cent is owned by local government, with the rest being split between the SSFA, Shetland Fish Processors' Association and Shetland Fishermen's Association. The SSQC inspectors make frequent and random checks at both farms and packing stations.

The Shetland Salmon Farmer's Association issues its own directives, which often, especially with regard to the use of chemicals, go well beyond the government's requirements. For instance, if, for any reason, antibiotics have been prescribed, a statutory period must elapse before the fish can be harvested. In Shetland this period is lengthened and then sample fish are tested and passed by SSQC as residue-free and suitable for harvesting.

The clean seas off Shetland help to keep down the incidence of sea lice, a natural parasite in wild fish, but when they do occur, and chemicals are used to eliminate them, similar safety precautions are adopted. Shetland is pioneering alternative methods of controlling sea lice, such as the use of natural cleaner fish like wrasse, and the farmers are aiming at the eventual elimination of all pesticides.

When questioned about the health of the North Atlantic, the farmers will say that it is both right and understandable to be concerned about pollution. To farm salmon you need clean sea and a clean sea bottom, and the first indication of anything being wrong is out-of-condition fish. In order to keep the natural balance of sea life the cages are moved periodically, and the sea bottom underneath the cages is examined annually by divers; they say marine life is healthy and prolific.

## Selling salmon

Five sales companies in Shetland handle most of the islands' salmon. They have multi-lingual staff and very sophisticated distribution systems, which enable them to deliver fresh salmon throughout the British Isles and Europe, or to airfreight it, in specially designed insulated boxes, to any part of the world.

The sales are collated by an impressive computer system. The staff can keep in constant touch with the packing stations and know the exact number and weight of fish being processed. The computer, which holds all details of every day's orders, will automatically reconcile supply with demand and point out if there is an over- or under-supply of any particular size of fish.

The main distribution point for the salmon is Aberdeen, and most of the fish goes there in cooled lorries on the overnight ferry from Lerwick. On arrival it is sorted and re-loaded, to depart within hours for destinations throughout Britain and the Continent. The farmers are proud of the fact that much of the salmon is delivered to consumer outlets within 48 hours of harvesting.

## Smoked Salmon and Gravad Lax

Shetland smoked salmon and gravad lax is, like everything else on the islands, produced to a high standard, with quality being the overriding criterion. Their smoked salmon is a good honest product; as one smoker puts it, he uses 'no additives and no fancy smoking with rum or whisky or brown sugar'.

With few trees on the islands, the wood needed for smoking is unobtainable on Shetland, and its three smokeries buy oak chippings from the Scottish mills, saying that the freshness and quality of the fish more than makes up for the inconvenience. The salmon for smoking is filleted at the packing station, and then taken to the smokery where, first of all, it is salted. The salt draws out the natural juices; if these juices are left, the fish remains too moist and it will stew rather than smoke. After a few hours the salt is washed off and the fillets are put into a light brine and left overnight. The proportion of salt to water is carefully gauged so that the fish retains maximum flavour.

The next morning the salmon is dried and, depending on the equipment, either hung or laid on trays in a special cold-smoking 'oven'. The oak chippings are lit, damped down to create the necessary smoke and the doors are shut. When ready, after 7-8 hours, the smoked salmon is packed according to each customer's requirements. Some is left as whole sides, but most is sold sliced – by hand – and packed in vacuum packs either as sides or in smaller quantities.

When there is time, the smoking ovens are used for herrings in the production of kippers. Shetland kippers are smoked without dyes, and although the colour might be a little drab to southern eyes, the taste is a revelation.

Not content with just smoking, the smokeries have also turned their attention to gravad lax, salmon cured with salt and flavoured with herbs. Yet again, an essential ingredient cannot be produced locally, and the dill has to be imported from Scotland.

East Voe, Quarff

Overleaf: Swarbacks Minn

Salmon farm, Selivoe

Salmon farm

Crofter Gilbert Hay, Omundsgarth, Sandsound

Overleaf: Gruting Voe

Salmon workboat

Repairing nets

Shetland gravad lax is light and fresh tasting and is sold unaccompanied by a little packet of sauce. The smokeries say that most packet sauces are far too strong for the delicate taste of gravad lax and, if they wish, people can make their own at home using fresh dill and a mild mustard.

Shetland smoked fish and gravad lax, like all the islands' other products, find their way round the world, and wherever you see fish with a Shetland label, you should buy it – it will be good.

## Shetland today and tomorrow

Shetland has always lived off fish. Commercial fishing started in the 14th century, and it is said that the sea is in every Shetlander's blood. Today, Shetland's rich fishing grounds yield lemon sole, turbot, halibut and monkfish as well as large quantities of herring and mackerel and, closer inshore, scallops, lobster and crab. Its modern fishing fleet is one of the most efficient and successful in Europe, with the industry employing some 600 men and utilizing around 100 boats. These boats vary from the small inshore ones used to gather scallops to large 70 metre trawlers. Even though each such trawler costs several million pounds, the skipper and crew still follow the age-old tradition of owning a share in their own boat.

Shetland Seafood Quality Control inspects and maintains standards within the sea fishing industry, and not just when the fish is landed from the boats. Some of the fish, like the salmon, is transported on the overnight ferry to Aberdeen, but much of it is processed on the islands. Some is frozen, some is canned, and some is cooked and sauced before being packed and frozen. As with salmon farming, the standards are high and fish sold with the SSQC label is all top quality.

At Scalloway on the west coast of Mainland, the North Atlantic Fisheries College has recently been built. This college brings together all facets of fishing in Shetland and is the centre for the study of aquaculture, fish processing and marine engineering. The Quality Control operation is also based at the college with up-to-date laboratories for disease diagnosis as well as for research and development. The college is also keeping an eye on the possibilities of farming other fish such as halibut, turbot and lemon sole.

Fish is part of Shetland life, and the fishing and salmon farming industries are almost entirely Shetland owned, with everyone sharing in both the ups and the downs. Shetlanders are thus never complacent and constantly look ahead with an eye to improvements, and to taking care of their islands and the environment. Salmon farmer Chris Young, who has led both the Association's environmental group and the Association itself, says: 'Look what has happened to the wild fish stocks: it is no longer possible to have a wild and uncontrolled environment. The farming of the sea and the management of the oceans is the only way forward.'

Shetlanders, with their commitment to their islands, to each other, and to the production of the very best, will be there, right out in front.

## Quantities

When you buy a whole fish it is usually weighed before gutting, and you are charged so much per pound or kilo based on that weight. As a result, it is much easier to use the complete weight as a guide to choosing the size of fish you want.

With a whole fish I generally allow 275-300g/9-10oz per person. This will yield portions of around 125-150g/4-5oz. If you are serving very little else you could increase the amount slightly or, if the table is going to be laden, cut it. It works out that for six people you will need a 1.8kg/4lb fish, for eight a 2.3kg/5lb fish, and one of 4kg/9lb will feed 16 people.

Salmon steaks sliced from the central part of the body are usually cooked and served individually as a main course. A steak will weigh 150-225g/5-7oz.

Salmon fillet is increasingly popular as it is bone-free and easily cut into a suitable size for one person. The tailpiece of the fish is frequently boned and used for individual pieces of fillet, or a whole filleted side can be cut into portions. For a first course you will need a piece of around 50g/2oz for each person, and for a main course a piece of 125-150g/4-5oz.

Escalopes are also frequently found, and you need the same weight per head as for fillet. Escalopes are sliced from a whole fillet in exactly the same way as smoked salmon. They can be used as they are, but remember that they will cook very quickly. They are more frequently used for dishes such as Carpaccio (page 85) or Saumon sur le plat (page 89), when the cut salmon is put between layers of greaseproof paper and beaten out to be almost transparent.

# BUYING AND
# PREPARING SALMON

It is worthwhile being fussy and insisting on the finest fresh salmon. The better the fish, the better your finished dish will be, so it is useful to be able to judge if the fish or cuts of fish are fresh, if they have been kept properly and are therefore worth purchasing.

If I am buying a whole fish, the first thing I always do is to touch it. Press your fingers lightly into the flesh, to check that it isn't soft or flabby; don't prod it too hard or the fishmonger won't be best pleased with you. If it feels cold and firm, your fingers hardly notice the scales and there is no mark on the salmon when you take them away, you have found a good fish.

The other classic ways of assessing a fish are to look at the gills: they should be dark red; the eyes: they should be bright; and to sniff: if the fish smells strong or unpleasant it is past its best.

Shetland salmon are tail-tagged with a best before date and information that the fish should be kept at no more than 2°C/36°F; providing this has been followed the quality of the fish will be excellent.

Buying pieces or cuts of salmon is more problematical than buying a whole fish. Cut-up and packaged supermarket salmon is inclined to be expensive, but it is usually very good, as it has been stored and handled correctly.

Buying cut fish from a fishmonger is usually cheaper and the quality is often absolutely excellent, especially from shops that cut on demand. If you find a helpful fishmonger with a clean shop or stall and good sparkling looking fish, use him; he will become a friend and be prepared to gut, cut up, fillet, skin or prepare the fish in whatever way you want. Sadly, not all fishmongers attain this standard, and if a shop looks messy or un-cared for, I would avoid it.

## Salmon and health

Research conducted in the 1970s showed that traditional fish eaters, such as the Eskimos, have a very low incidence of heart attacks. Further studies have demonstrated that the Japanese, with their fish-rich diet, also suffer little from heart disease and, at the same time, have the greatest life expectancy of any developed nation.

Fish is a high-protein food that is low in carbohydrates and has very little saturated fat. As is now well known, fish also contains substances called omega-3 or long chain polyunsaturates. These exist in all fish, but as they are present only in the fat content of the fish, they appear in greater volume in oily fish such as herring, mackerel and salmon.

The consumption of omega-3 polyunsaturates is instrumental in the prevention of many diseases. They are prescribed for the prevention of heart disease, to reduce the risk of complications following heart surgery, to suppress the side effects of certain drugs, and to help reduce high blood pressure. Relief can also be obtained for conditions such as eczema, asthma, rheumatism, arthritis and inflammation of the joints.

It is fascinating to know that a large part of the grey matter of the human brain consists of one of these omega-3 polyunsaturates, DHA. The reason for its presence is as yet unknown, but there is evidence that humans require these substances, and since they cannot be created by our bodies, we need to eat food in which they are present. I am sure that Hercule Poirot enjoyed reviving his little grey cells with a perfectly poached salmon steak!

## Storing salmon

When you get the fish home, the quicker you cook and eat it the better it will be, but if you are going to keep it, even for an hour or two, put it into the refrigerator. Salmon keeps best as a gutted whole fish, and if you have to buy the fish a day or so before you plan to cook it, it is better, if you want steaks or fillets, to cut it up yourself. It is not too difficult to do and on pages 21-22 I give a few basic instructions.

If you are going to freeze the fish, do it immediately you get it home. Set your freezer to a low temperature and wrap the fish in two layers of foil. Keep it for no more than a month and, if possible, defrost it slowly in the bottom of the fridge.

## Scaling

If you are going to cook the fish whole and then skin it, or remove the skin before you cook it, there is no need to scale it.

If you plan to cut the fish into steaks or to fillet it, and cook it with the skin still on, it should be scaled. It can be a messy job, and is best done on several sheets of newspaper and, if possible, out of doors.

Use a fish scaler or a serrated knife and scrape away the scales. Work against the grain: from tail to head. When you have loosened or removed all the scales, wash the fish under a running cold tap, again working against the grain, and using a colander or something similar to catch any remaining scales.

## Gutting

To gut the fish, use a heavy sharp knife or a pair of scissors, and being careful not to insert the knife or scissor blade too deeply, cut along the belly from the gills to the ventral opening. Remove the innards and discard.

The gills, if left, will give a very bitter taste to any poaching liquid, so cut them out using a pair of stout scissors.

Thoroughly wash the fish under cold running water. With the end of a teaspoon, or something similar, scrape away any traces of blood on the backbone, wash it away and, using paper towels, dry the inside of the fish.

## Cutting steaks

Steaks can be cut all down the fish from just behind the head to where it starts to taper for the tail. The tail is usually boned and cut into fillets.

Use a heavy knife and cut the fish into even slices. You may need a cleaver to cut through the backbone.

Cut salmon should never be washed, as the water will wash away the juices and flavour. If a steak or a cut piece of salmon needs tidying up or cleaning, pat it all over with a piece of lightly dampened kitchen paper.

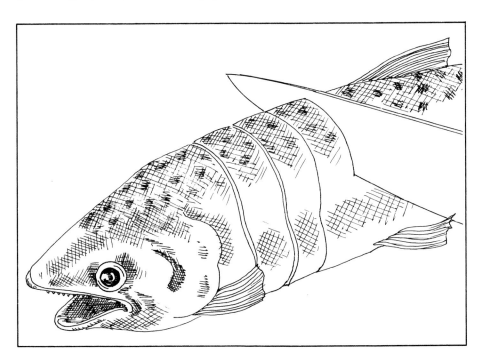

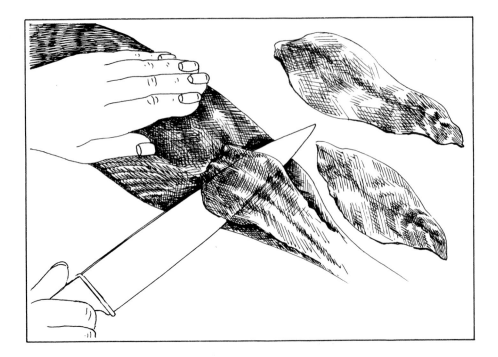

## Cutting escalopes

Escalopes are cut from the fish in much the same way as smoked salmon is sliced, and you will need a whole fillet or side of salmon. The colder the fish, the easier it is to cut. The escalopes need to be paper thin, and unless you are a real whizz at cutting it, you will need to beat it out with a rolling pin. Any leftover fish may be used in another recipe.

## Filleting

Whole skinned salmon fillets are used for Salmon en croûte (page 120). Many other dishes call for small individual pieces of salmon fillet. These are usually taken from the tail section, but they can be a piece of middle cut that has been boned and skinned.

To fillet a whole salmon: put the fish on its side and using a strong, very sharp knife, cut down behind the head to the backbone. Follow the bone formation and keep the knife angled towards the mouth of the fish.

Slice down the centre back of the fish, keeping the knife flat and directly on top of the backbone. Pulling the fillet up as you go along, cut again over the rib cage from head to tail, and the whole fillet will come away from the fish. Turn the fish over and remove the second fillet in exactly the same way.

Lay the fillets out flat, and using a pair of tweezers, pull out the pin bones that lie along the length of the fillet. You can find them by running your fingers over the fish.

To fillet a tailpiece of salmon, start at the tail end and cut off each fillet.

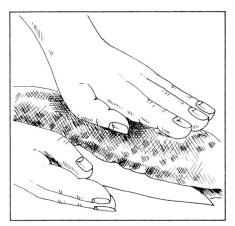
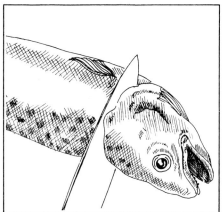
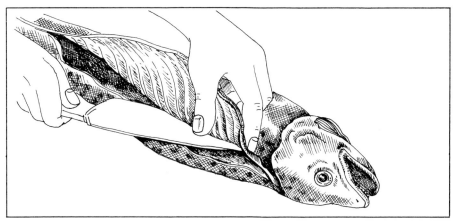
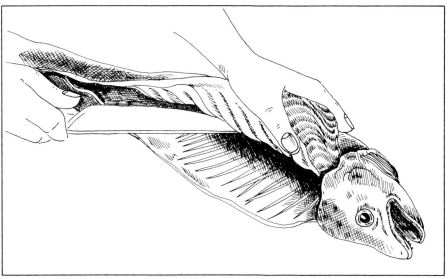

## Skinning a fillet

Put the fillet, skin side down, on to a work surface, and start by separating the fish from the skin by making a small cut at the tail end.

Hold on to the skin; if it is slippery dip your fingers in salt or use a cloth. Pull on the skin and use a sawing action, keeping the knife flat so that it cuts through neither the skin nor the flesh, and you will find that the fillet easily comes away.

## Boning a whole fish

A fish needs to be boned if it is going to be stuffed. You can then produce a beautiful whole salmon, which can be cut right through and served in slices, fish, stuffing and all (see the recipes on pages 122 and 124).

After the fish has been gutted, cut off the fins. Lay the fish on its side and using a sharp knife, lengthen the belly opening on one side of the backbone right down to the tail. With the aid of a knife or pair of scissors, release the rib bones lining the upper fillet, and if they are embedded in the flesh leave them for the time being and cut them off at the backbone. Turn the fish over and repeat the operation on the other side.

Using a stout pair of kitchen scissors, cut through the backbone at both the head and the tail. Hold on to the backbone at the head end and pull it up and away from the fish, being careful not to tear the flesh and to cut off any further bones that are buried in the flesh. Find the cut bones by rubbing your fingers down the inside of the fish and remove them with tweezers.

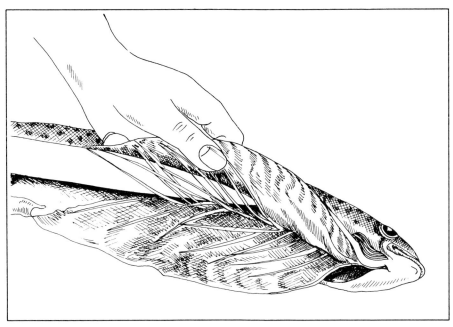

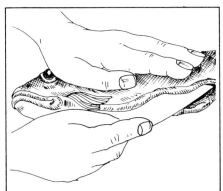

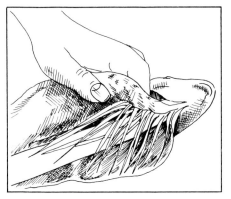

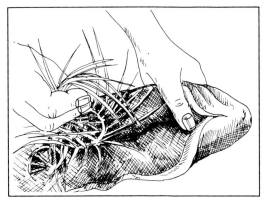

# COOKING SALMON

Salmon, to be eaten hot or cold, as a whole fish or in smaller cuts, can be cooked in many different ways. This section deals with all the well known, and some of the less well known cooking methods. Each method comes with suggestions as to which cut or piece of salmon to use and approximate timings. Timings inevitably vary according to the thickness of the fish and the exact temperature of the oven, grill or pan, but I have found that these work. Overcooked salmon is a disaster: it becomes dry, tasteless and thoroughly dull, so time it and watch it very carefully.

The method you use is a matter of choice, but it is worth considering whether the fish is to be eaten hot or cold and the butter or sauce or sauces you plan to serve.

## Cooking whole salmon

A whole salmon, served either hot or cold, can undoubtedly make a dramatic centre-piece to a table. For a party, and especially for large numbers, the choice is frequently for a cold fish, skinned and served just as it is, or decorated with cucumber, aspic or in another imaginative way to match the occasion.

If you own a fish kettle the cooking of the fish is simplicity itself, but it is an expensive piece of equipment to buy, and you may feel that you don't entertain enough to justify it. Some kitchen shops hire them out, or otherwise you may be able to borrow one from a friend. Without a fish kettle the solution generally put forward is to cook the fish in foil and, if you are going to eat it hot, this is a good method.

Place the salmon on a piece of well buttered foil, spread it with lemon slices and herbs, moisten with a splash of wine, then wrap it up and cook it in the oven. Serve the juices from the packet with the fish or use them in the sauce that accompanies it. Cooking the fish in the same way and then serving it cold is something that, to me, does not quite work, as salmon to be eaten cold is infinitely better if it is cooked in water, or a court bouillon, and without any fat or oil. If you simply wrap the salmon in a plain piece of foil and cook it in the oven you will land up with a very dry and unappetising fish, but if you wrap it and cook it in water or steam, it will remain moist and be very good. You can put the wrapped fish either in a fish kettle, or (and don't laugh) into the dishwasher (see pages 27 and 30).

My local fishmonger, John Nicolson of Chiswick, who sells beautiful cold dressed salmon, came up with another way round the problem, and that is to curl the salmon into an enormous foil tent, add some water, heat it in the oven, and eat it hot or leave it, as in a fish kettle, to cool in its own steam. A curled fish is also wonderfully decorative as you have the bonus of being able to fill the centre with greenery, herbs and/or flowers.

Sophie Grigson sent me a lovely bunch of spring flowers to thank me for my help raising money for a gastronomic library being established in memory of her mother, the great Jane Grigson. They arrived at a propitious moment, and looked wonderful adorning a curled salmon for a Sunday lunch party: I felt that Jane would have liked the result.

## Using a fish kettle

Fish kettles come in sizes from 40-100cm/16-40 inches. Select a kettle to comfortably fit your fish. The fish should be neither squashed nor floundering about.

You can poach the fish in a court bouillon (see page 38), a flavoured stock (see below), or plain water, but the liquid should always be unsalted. This is for two reasons: firstly, salt is inclined to stiffen the flesh of salmon, and secondly, if the stock is to be used for a sauce or for aspic, you will need an unsalted liquid that can be seasoned and balanced after it has been boiled down and reduced. I tend to poach salmon in plain water or a lightly flavoured stock and to make a court bouillon only when I plan to use it afterwards for a sauce, a soup, or for aspic.

For a flavoured stock, to the water in the fish kettle I add half a bottle of white wine, some peppercorns, a quartered lemon, a small bunch of parsley and possibly, depending on the sauce I plan to serve, another herb, such as tarragon.

You can judge the amount of court bouillon you will need by putting the fish into the fish kettle, pouring in enough water to just cover it, then removing the fish and measuring the amount of water.

## Cooking a salmon to be eaten cold

A fish can lose its shape in cooking, so make sure that it has its belly down with the flaps tucked underneath before placing it on the rack in the fish kettle. If it is a very large fish it is best to wrap it in muslin first.

Cover the salmon with the poaching liquid: cold water, a lightly flavoured stock or a court bouillon (see page 38), and bring it slowly up to simmering point. Let the liquid bubble two or three times, then put on the lid, remove the fish kettle from the heat and leave until the liquid is cold. Your fish will be perfectly cooked.

An alternative is to wrap the fish in foil and cook it in water in a fish kettle. Wrap your fish tightly in two layers of foil, place it in the fish kettle, cover with water, bring it slowly to the boil and let it bubble gently for 2-3 minutes. Put on the lid, remove the fish kettle from the heat and leave until cold.

## Cooking a salmon to be eaten hot

First measure your fish at the thickest point to gauge cooking time. Put the fish on a rack in the fish kettle, cover it with cold water, stock or a court bouillon and bring it slowly to the boil, allowing it to take around 20 minutes. Let it simmer gently for 3 minutes per centimetre/7 minutes per inch thickness, then take it from the heat and leave for 15 minutes before removing the fish from the liquid.

Fish differ in shape and thickness, but you won't go far wrong if you follow the timings in the box below.

| Weight of fish | Simmering time |
| --- | --- |
| up to 2.7kg/6lb | 8 minutes |
| 2.7-3.6kg/6-8lb | 10 minutes |
| 3.6-4.5kg/8-10lb | 12 minutes |
| 4.5-5.5kg/10/12lb | 15 minutes |

In all cases leave the salmon in the hot liquid for 15 minutes after the fish kettle has been removed from the heat. You can then skin the fish, possibly bone it, and place it on a serving platter. Surround it with lemon wedges, watercress or cucumber and serve it with a sauce or sauces of your choice.

## Skinning the salmon

Whether you are serving salmon hot or cold, it is much nicer to present a skinned fish. A fish to be eaten hot must be skinned quickly, the moment it comes from the cooking liquid.

Lay a large sheet of greaseproof paper on your work surface and dampen it with water. Lift the poaching rack from the fish kettle, and hold it so that as much liquid as possible is drained from the salmon. Transfer the fish to the greaseproof paper and pull out and discard the fins and the little bones attached to them. Using a spatula or table knife, peel off the skin. It will come away easily, and when you have done one side, use the paper to roll the fish over so that you can peel off the remaining skin.

Along the backbone and over the sides the fish will probably have a brown creamy curd, and for appearances' sake this should be removed, by scraping gently with the knife or spatula. Use the greaseproof paper to lift the salmon and then gently roll it on to the serving dish.

## Boning salmon

This is normally done only with a cold salmon, but there is nothing to stop you doing it with a hot one, except that it takes time. The fish will be warm and not hot when served, but I think this seldom matters with poached salmon.

Start by skinning the salmon and placing it on its side on the serving platter or board. Take a sharp pointed knife and cut the flesh free round the salmon's head and tail, and then cut down between the two fillets along the centre of the fish. Cut down along the centre back of the fish, keeping the knife horizontal and just above the backbone; you should feel the fillet coming away from the bone. When the back fillet is free, use a fish slice or spatula to lift it and put it on a sheet of damp greaseproof paper. Should the fillet be too long, cut it cleanly into two or three and lift it off the fish a piece at a time.

Use the knife to free the front fillet and, in the same way, lift it from the fish. Using a pair of strong scissors cut through the bone at the tail end. Hold on to the bone, gently pull it up from the fish and use a knife to cut off any flesh that sticks to it. Finally snip through the head end and throw the bone out.

With the aid of the greaseproof paper, lift the fillets and lay them back in position. Use a spatula to smooth down any cracks and a piece of kitchen paper to clean up the plate.

## Decorating the fish

I am not going to give long descriptions of how to twist your lemon slices, or turn your tomatoes into roses, as I think that decoration is very personal and often, the simpler it is, the prettier it is. I will, however, give instructions for using aspic as a coating. It is a classic way of serving a salmon, especially one decorated with cucumber slices, and it is also the best way of hiding any broken flesh or imperfections.

Follow the instructions on page 39 to make the aspic jelly. Peel a cucumber, leaving some strips of skin, cut it in half lengthwise, and then, in a food processor, or using a very sharp knife, slice it very thinly. Put the slices into a bowl of iced salted water. Leave them for 30 minutes, then drain and pat dry.

Arrange the cucumber slices to resemble scales, all down the fish. Chill the fish, either in the refrigerator, or, for a few minutes, in the deep freeze, then remove any moisture by patting all over with a piece of kitchen paper.

Have a bowl of cold water with some ice cubes floating in it. Pour some lukewarm aspic jelly into a metal bowl and stand it in the cold water. Stir frequently, but very gently or bubbles will form, until it thickens and is syrupy. If it starts to set or go lumpy you will have to melt it again by putting the base of the bowl into hot water.

When the consistency is similar to that of raw egg white, dribble the aspic from a spoon on to the fish. To have as much control as possible, keep the spoon as close to the fish as you can. The aspic will spread over the cucumber and quickly set. You may have to re-melt the bowl of jelly as you go along, but, when used at the right consistency, one layer of aspic should be enough; you want to achieve a nice glisten rather than a thick covering.

If you like, pour any leftover aspic round the fish and leave it to set. Otherwise pour it on to a sheet of greaseproof paper and then, when it has set, chop it with a wet knife and spoon it round the fish.

Chill or keep cold until needed, then serve with mayonnaise or other sauce of your choice.

I found another way of using cucumber and aspic in a book published in 1933: *Fifty Ways of Cooking Fish*, by Mrs Elsie Turner.

For a 5lb fish take two cucumbers, peel them, cut them lengthwise into quarters and remove the seeds. Cut the flesh into julienne strips. Plunge the strips into boiling salted water, cook for two minutes, drain and dry in a clean tea towel. Melt 4oz butter and stir into it the juice of half a lemon, a tablespoon each of chopped tarragon and chopped chervil or parsley, and the cucumber.

Place the cooked skinned fish on a dish, arrange the cucumber round it, refrigerate until very cold and cover with aspic jelly.

## A curled salmon

Follow the instructions on page 20 for preparing the fish. Set the oven to 190°C/375°F/gas 5.

Take two very large sheets of foil and lay them, at right angles to each other, on a baking tin. Place a 900ml-1.2 litre/1½-2 pint pudding basin upside down in the middle. Take a long piece of string, double it, put one end through the gills of the salmon, and tie it leaving two long ends. Tie one of the ends to the tail, again leaving an end of reasonable length.

The next stage is easier if you have somebody to help you. Put the salmon on the foil and, with its back upwards, curl it round the pudding basin. Take the two loose ends and tie them, and pull, tying the final knot when the salmon is in a tight circle round the pudding basin.

Turn up the edges of the foil and pour 300ml/½ pint water, or mixed water and wine, over the fish. Add, if you like, some lemon slices, peppercorns and parsley. Pull up the foil and seal it, opposite piece to opposite piece, into a tent shape.

Put into the oven and cook for 25 minutes plus 5 minutes per 500g/1lb, then remove from the oven. If the salmon is to be served hot, let it stand for 15 minutes before unwrapping and skinning; if cold, leave in the tent until the fish and liquid have cooled.

Unwrap the fish, cut away the string and skin it. Using the foil, transfer it to a serving dish – a big meat platter would be suitable. Scrape the brown curd from the backbone and the sides of the fish.

Cover the groove left by the curd with a line of watercress, parsley or cucumber slices. A cold fish can, of course, be set with a layer of aspic. Fill the centre hole and decorate the fish in any way that takes your fancy.

## Cooking salmon in the dishwasher

A gimmick – well, yes! But one that works. While researching for this book, I met somebody who cooks a great many salmon, and always does it in the dishwasher. She says they are moist, skin and bone easily and as a 2.3kg/5lb fish takes a whole cycle, there is no worry over calculating cooking time according to thickness. She told me that she had experimented with other foods and that trout overcooked and vegetables didn't cook at all!

You can eat dishwasher-cooked salmon either hot or cold. If you plan to eat it cold, wrap it in foil without oil or butter, but add, if you like, some lemon slices or herbs. For a salmon to be eaten hot, use butter or oil to grease the inside of the foil, and put a little more butter inside and on top of the fish. Again, you can add lemon slices, herbs and possibly a splash of wine.

I would recommend that before you cook the salmon you run the dishwasher, when empty, through a short programme. You will them know that the water is clean, should your package split or develop a hole.

Wash a 2.3kg/5lb salmon both inside and out, then wrap it in two, or even three, separate layers of foil; use large pieces and be extra careful to seal it well and fold over the joins in the foil at least twice. You can then, for extra protection, put the foil parcel in a plastic bag, but be quite sure that all the air is expelled, and seal the opening tightly.

Place the salmon on the top rack of the dishwasher, and if the spikes get in the way you can put the parcel on a wire cake rack, or something similar, to give it some protection.

Remembering not to add any powder, run the long hot cycle, which takes around an hour and a half and heats the water to 65°C/150°F in most machines. When it has finished, leave the salmon, without opening the door, for 15 minutes.

If you are going to eat the fish hot, take it from the dishwasher immediately the 15 minutes are up, snip off a corner of foil and drain out the juices. Season them and serve as a sauce. Unwrap the parcel, carefully skin the salmon and serve immediately. If the salmon is to be eaten cold, leave it to cool in the parcel, then unwrap it, and skin and possibly bone it (see page 28).

## Cooking in foil

I have said elsewhere that I don't think of foil as a replacement for a fish kettle, but a hot salmon from a foil parcel that is also bursting with herbs, lemon slices and wine is delicious. Cook it slowly according to the instructions below, and 10 minutes before you think it might be ready, check it. Use a sharp knife to see if the fish is coming away from the bone, and if it needs further cooking, re-seal the parcel and return it to the oven.

Take a large sheet of foil and smear the inside generously with butter, or oil it well. Place the salmon on it, season it inside and out, and tuck some slices of lemon and sprigs of herbs inside it. Dot the fish with a little more butter and, having lifted up the sides of the foil, pour a glass or so of white wine over the top. Wrap it up into a loose parcel, but not one that is over-large and balloon-like, and seal the edges well by folding them together two or three times.

If your fish is too big for your oven you can cut it through into two or three pieces. Make each piece into a separate parcel, and after cooking, reassemble the fish on a serving dish. All the joins and cuts can be covered and hidden with slices of cucumber or sprigs of watercress.

Preheat your oven to 160°C/325°F/gas 3 and cook a fish of 2.3kg/5lb or over for 8 minutes per 500g/1lb. For a smaller fish or pieces of fish increase the cooking time to 10 minutes per 500g/1lb.

Leave the parcel to rest for a few minutes after removing it from the oven. Snip off a corner of the foil and drain off the liquid; it will make a good sauce. Unwrap the fish, skin the top, turn it, skin the other side, and then use the foil to slide it on to a serving dish.

If the fish has been cooked in two or three separate parcels, follow the directions above and slide the pieces in the right order on to the dish. Cover the joins with cucumber, watercress or herbs.

## The microwave

Microwaves are not the answer to everything, but used selectively they are, in my opinion, extremely good. If you want a perfectly poached piece of salmon, for eating either hot or cold, cook it in the microwave. It will remain moist, be very tasty and, provided it is not overcooked, the flesh will hold together nicely. This is not a microwave book, but in some of the recipes, and when it has seemed to be a sensible alternative, I have suggested using it.

A whole fish is too big for a microwave, and large centre cuts with a thickness of more than 10cm/4 inches will not cook evenly. However, the microwave is excellent for a tailpiece or any of the smaller cuts and is wonderfully quick if you need a small piece of cooked fish for something like the Salmon paste (page 81) or the Lasagne (page 136).

If you are cooking a piece of salmon that is more than 2.5cm/1 inch thick, you will find it cooks more evenly if you stop and turn it half way through, but with the thinner cuts and if your oven has a turntable, this should not be necessary. In order to make sure that the fish does not overcook, you may find it helpful to set the oven time for 30 seconds less than you think will be needed. Having checked, you can, if necessary, return the dish to the oven. The cooking time is governed by the thickness and quantity of fish; the more steaks or pieces of fillet you put in the oven, the longer they will take. After removing the fish from the oven, leave it to stand for 3-5 minutes; you will find that it will continue cooking, so remove it when still slightly underdone and pink in the middle.

I use a 650 watt oven and the timings below are based on that; if yours has a different wattage, alter them slightly. Supermarket packets of salmon often suggest that in a 650

| Fish | Quantity | Cooking time |
|---|---|---|
| 175g/6oz steaks | 1 | 3 minutes |
| | 2 | 4½ minutes |
| | 4 | 6 minutes |
| 150-175g/5-6oz pieces of fillet | 1 | 2½ minutes |
| | 2 | 3½ minutes |
| | 4 | 5 minutes |
| 375-625g/12oz-1¼lb tailpiece | 1 | 3½-5 minutes |

Hi-technology sea cage

Fish farmer, John Ratter

watt oven the fish should be cooked at 80% power, but I have always, and successfully, used full power.

Place the fish in a china or plastic dish, and if you are cooking several pieces at once, arrange them like the spokes of a wheel, with the thickest part outwards. Sprinkle with 1-2 tablespoons water, depending on the amount of fish you are cooking. Cover. If using a lid, leave an air vent, if using clingfilm, pierce it with a knife in two or three places.

## Steamed salmon

Steaming is an ideal method of cooking fish because of the constant temperature as well as the moisture. Use steaks or fillets or, if you have a very large steamer, you could cook a whole fish. Place the fish directly on the bottom of the steaming basket or, like the Chinese, put it on a plate or dish, cover and then place in the basket. You can also put the fish on a bed of herbs or vegetables; see Salmon with samphire on page 99.

The cooking time is, as always, dictated by the thickness of the fish. In the recipes I give approximate timings only, because although the temperature of the steam will remain constant, the amount of steam will not. As a guide, if you are cooking directly in the basket, allow 7 minutes per 2.5cm/1 inch, measured at the thickest part of the fish. If the fish is placed on a bed of vegetables you will need to slightly increase the cooking time. For a piece of fish on a covered plate or dish allow 4 minutes per centimetre or 10 minutes per inch.

## Poached cuts of salmon

Salmon steaks, pieces of fillet or larger middle cuts can all be poached and eaten hot, or left until cold.

Choose a pan into which the salmon will fit comfortably and, if possible, fill with enough flavoured liquid or court bouillon (see page 38) to cover the piece or pieces of salmon. Bring the liquid to just below boiling point, put in the salmon and maintain the liquid at a gentle simmer. The time needed is exactly the same as for a whole fish: just under 3 minutes per centimetre or 7 minutes per inch thickness. If the fish isn't competely covered by the liquid, you will need to turn it halfway through cooking and add another minute to the time.

When the cooking time is up, take the pan from the heat and, if it is to be served hot, leave the fish to rest for 5 minutes before removing it from the pan. If it is to be eaten cold, leave it until the liquid has cooled.

## Pan-fried salmon

You can pan-fry any cut of salmon: escalopes, pieces of fillet or steaks. The cooked fish will be almost indistinguishable from a piece that has been grilled, and can be served with lemon juice, a flavoured butter, a separate sauce or one that uses the cooking juices in the pan. I give several examples on pages 106-108.

Very often I read recipes for pan-frying fish, or sometimes meat, that recommend using a nonstick frying pan without butter or oil. This does work, but I have great respect for my nonstick pans, and heating the pan and cooking without any lubricant is something I avoid, so I use just enough butter or oil to film the bottom of the pan. There is no need to use a nonstick pan, but unless you have a pan that is an old friend and very well seasoned it does make it easier.

If possible, use salmon that has been out of the fridge for an hour or so and is at room temperature. Cold food takes longer to cook, is more difficult to cook evenly and is much more likely to dry up and develop a hard crust on the outside.

Lightly season the fish with salt and pepper. Put 15g/½oz butter or 1 tablespoon sunflower or olive oil (a fruity one gives the salmon a good flavour) into the pan. Preheat the pan until a drop of water shows signs of sizzling on coming into contact with the metal.

For a thin piece of salmon, put in the fish, and cook for 1-2 minutes each side. Test it by seeing if a fork will slide easily into the flesh, and if not, cook for a little longer.

For a thick piece, put the fish in the pan, cook for 1 minute each side, then turn down the heat and cover with a lid or a piece of foil and continue cooking for a further 2-5 minutes, turning the fish once more. Check with a fork, and with salmon steaks make sure that the flesh will come away easily from the bone.

## Grilled salmon

Use either steaks or pieces of fillet. Bring them to room temperature before grilling or the extra cooking time will be inclined to make the outside hard and the fish dry.

There are several ways of keeping the flesh moist. You can brush the salmon with oil or butter; melted butter is particularly good. Brush it fairly generously over the cut fish and then leave it to stand for 20 minutes or so before grilling.

If you don't want to use extra fat, sprinkle the salmon with salt 2-3 minutes before putting it under the grill. The salt will make the juices start to run and they, in turn, will prevent the outside from drying.

Preheat your grill. Place the salmon on a rack and, if you are using butter, put a dish or foil under the rack to catch the juices. Put the salmon 5-7.5cm/2-3 inches from the grill and turn after 2-3 minutes. After a further 2-3 minutes, check to see if it is cooked. As always, the exact time needed depends on the thickness of the salmon.

You can grill it without turning it, but the height of flame is then crucial, as the underside needs to be just cooked without the top becoming overdone.

## Barbecued salmon

Salmon is good on the barbecue, and is best cooked quickly over the glowing coals. It can be marinated and then grilled, or cooked simply brushed with oil and sprinkled with fresh chopped dill or fennel. Put the stalks on to the barbecue just as you start cooking the fish.

When barbecueing pieces of fillet, leave the skin on, or the fish will fall apart. Rub some salt into the skin, and when cooked it will be lovely and crunchy. Brush the steaks, or pieces of fillet, lightly with oil, lay directly on the hot oiled grid, and cook for 2-3 minutes each side. Serve as they are or with a flavoured butter. For the real barbecue flavour, use the sauce on page 65. Marinate the fish by brushing some of the sauce over it several hours before cooking. Keep the remainder of the sauce and hand it round with the fish.

A whole barbecued salmon is a treat indeed. To turn it over, and eventually remove the fish from the barbecue, you will need to use something to hold it: a double-sided hinged grill, especially made for barbecues, is the best, but failing that, you can cook the fish in foil.

Prepare the salmon by making three or four diagonal cuts through the skin on each side and painting them, and the inside of the fish, with the barbecue sauce or with oil and chopped herbs. Put the fish into the double-sided grill or wrap it in foil, making sure the ends are properly secured. Slash the foil at an angle once or twice down each side, but be careful not to cut right round.

Cook the fish over a large quantity of hot coals, turning it two or three times. It will take 15-20 minutes a side and rather longer if the barbecue cools down.

# STOCKS, SAUCES AND ACCOMPANIMENTS

## Stock

Good stock really is worthwhile, and provided you have the right ingredients to hand, it is not difficult to make.

I give a recipe for a salmon stock, a vegetable one and a classic fish stock made with the bones and trimmings of white fish. Mixed bones are usually used, and the stock will be better textured and firmer with the inclusion of some bones of flat fish or turbot, as they yield a lot of gelatine. Having made and strained the stock, you can boil it down to the concentration you require, but remember not to salt it until it has been reduced.

In many supermarkets it is now possible to buy high quality fish stock that can be frozen for storage. It is also possible to buy passable cubes, but they all contain a high proportion of salt, so use them prudently so that if the stock is reduced to make a sauce it will not be too salty.

## Salmon Stock

A straightforward stock that uses the bones and head of the salmon. If you have an obliging fishmonger who will also give you a few bones or trimmings of white fish, the stock will be improved.

HEAD, TAIL AND BONES OF FISH
½ ONION
1 SMALL CARROT
4 PEPPERCORNS
A FEW PARSLEY STALKS
BAYLEAF
SOME THYME, OR OTHER AVAILABLE HERB, OR A BOUQUET GARNI
175ml/6 fl.oz WHITE WINE (OPTIONAL)

Make sure that the gills have been removed from the salmon head and that the bones are free of blood.

Put everything into a saucepan, cover with 1.2 litres/2 pints water, and bring slowly to the boil. Skim if necessary, then leave it to simmer fast for 20 minutes. Strain, and if you want a more concentrated stock, pour it back into the pan and boil down to the required strength.

Once made the stock can be frozen.

# Fish Stock

A stock made with white fish is often known by its French name *fumet*. I looked up fumet in my dictionary and one of the definitions given is 'pleasant smell of food cooking'. Fish stock can smell 'pleasant', but it must be quickly made or the pleasantness will go and the resulting stock will be bitter.

750g/1½lb FISH BONES AND TRIMMINGS
1 ONION, SLICED
½ STALK CELERY OR ½ TSP CELERY SALT
BOUQUET GARNI
6 PEPPERCORNS
1 tbsp WHITE WINE VINEGAR
250ml/8 fl oz WHITE WINE (OPTIONAL)
ZEST OF ½ LEMON

Wash the bones well, cut them into pieces and put them and all the other ingredients into a large (non-aluminium) pan. Add just enough water to cover, 900ml-1.2 litres/1½-2 pints. Bring to the boil, skimming frequently, then simmer fast for 20 minutes. Strain and cool, or re-boil and reduce to the concentration you require.

Use exactly the same ingredients to make fish stock in a microwave. Put them all in a large bowl and just cover with water, leaving some headspace. Cover and microwave for 20 minutes. Strain and use as required.

37

# Vegetable Stock

If you don't have any fish bones this makes a perfectly adequate substitute. The ingredients and flavourings can be varied according to what is avilable or to what sauce you plan to make.

1 ONION OR LEEK, SLICED
1 CARROT, SLICED
1 STALK CELERY, SLICED
A LITTLE TURNIP, SLICED (OPTIONAL)
PARSLEY STALKS AND/OR OTHER FRESH HERBS
A LITTLE LEMON ZEST
CLOVE GARLIC
BLACK PEPPERCORNS

Put everything in a saucepan with 600ml/1 pint water, bring to the boil and simmer for 30-40 minutes. Strain and use as required.

# Court Bouillon

Court bouillon is the lightly flavoured liquid in which fish is poached. For a large fish kettle you will probably need to make at least twice the quantity I give here (see page 27) but if you are poaching just one salmon steak you will need about a quarter of the quantity. Whatever your need the recipe remains the same: just double it, halve it or whatever.

1 litre/1¾ pints WATER
300 ml/½ pint WHITE WINE, OR 75ml/3fl oz WHITE WINE VINEGAR
OR LEMON JUICE
1 LARGE ONION, SLICED
1 LARGE CARROT, SLICED
1 – 2 STALKS CELERY
BOUQUET GARNI
PINCH SALT

Put everything into the fish kettle or a large pan, bring to the boil and simmer, uncovered, for 20-30 minutes. Leave until quite cool and strain or not, as you wish.

# Aspic Jelly

Make aspic jelly using fish stock or the court bouillon from poaching the salmon.

Boil down the strained stock until you have no more than 600ml/1 pint. If you are using court bouillon, reduce the liquid to about half or one third, use 600ml/1 pint for the aspic jelly and keep or freeze the rest.

Leave the reduced liquid until cold and then test its consistency to judge how much gelatine will be needed to achieve a proper set. Pour a spoonful of stock on to a plate and cool in the fridge or freezer, then test the set with your finger. If it has set lightly you will probably need to use 7g/½ packet of gelatine, or if it is still very liquid, 14g/1 packet.

Clarify the stock, if you are going to. To do this, add a crushed shell and the white of 1 egg to the stock and bring it, whisking occasionally, to the boil. Boil for 5 minutes, when a white foam will form on the top, then remove from the heat and leave for 10 minutes. Strain through a muslin-lined sieve and reheat before adding the gelatine.

Soften the gelatine in a little water and stir it into the hot, but not boiling, stock. Cool, but not so much that it sets, and use as required.

# Sauces and Accompaniments

'It is the duty of a good sauce,' wrote the editor of the *Almanach des Gourmands* 'to insinuate itself all round.' I do agree with him, and one of the joys of salmon is that it lends itself so well to insinuation.

The sauce you choose to serve with salmon is often the pivot for the whole meal; add a butter or a sauce to a piece of perfectly cooked salmon and the food starts to light up and the meal to find its direction.

This chapter has recipes for all the classic sauces and follows them with ideas and suggestions for variations, using different herbs or flavourings. The other sauces may not be classics, but all of them 'insinuate' themselves well, and they extend and widen the selection. With most of the sauces it is fairly obvious if they are suitable for hot or cold salmon, but some will go with either, and I have pointed this out in the relevant recipes.

Unfortunately for the health-conscious, it is difficult to make a sauce without using butter, eggs or cream, and all the classics include one, two, or all three of them. I have, where appropriate, cut down on the amounts, and I have also included one or two of the less rich sauces, such as Sauce bâtarde. Another solution is to restrict the amount of sauce and serve no more than a tablespoonful for each person. If you want to cut your fat intake right down, you can make one of the butters substituting margarine. In the main part of the book I have also given several recipes that use little or no butter or cream.

I finish the chapter with a few cucumber salads, for even if cucumber has been used to decorate a cold salmon, in my opinion a cucumber salad is an essential addition to the table.

# Butters

The easiest way of serving hot salmon is to sprinkle it with salt and freshly ground black pepper, squeeze on a little lemon juice and top it with a pat of butter, which will enticingly melt its way into the flesh.

Carry the idea one stage further and top your piece of salmon with a flavoured butter. This will add to both the taste and the visual appeal of the dish: as the butter melts it will leave behind it a layer of green herbs or other coloured flavouring.

Flavoured butters are all made in the same way, using soft butter and beating it into the other ingredients until everything is amalgamated. Wrap the butter in foil, press it into a sausage shape, and refrigerate until needed. To serve, just cut off a pat and put it on top of the hot fish.

For the simpler butters I give quantities using 50g/2oz butter, which is enough to top four salmon steaks or pieces of fillet. However, it is too small a quantity for a normal sized food processor bowl, so make it using a bowl and a wooden spoon.

## Beurre Maître d'Hôtel (Parsley Butter)

A classic, and one that is traditionally eaten with grilled fish. It is also good put on top of the new potatoes that may be accompanying the salmon.

125g/4oz UNSALTED BUTTER
3 tbsp CHOPPED PARSLEY
1 tbsp LEMON JUICE (OR TO TASTE)
SALT AND PEPPER

## Hazelnut and Honey Butter

For those with a sweet tooth.

Using a food processor, grind 1 tbsp hazelnuts. Mix them and 1 tsp each runny honey and balsamic or sherry vinegar into 50g/2oz softened butter. Season to taste.

# Herb Butters

Herbs other than parsley can be used in butters, either on their own, or mixed. If you are using one of the stronger herbs such as tarragon, or green leaves such as watercress, spinach or sorrel, it is better to blanch them before use. Put the herb or picked-over leaves in boiling water for a minute, drain and pat dry on a kitchen cloth, then chop and amalgamate with the other ingredients. If you want something more robust, add a little finely chopped shallot or garlic.

# Citrus Butters

A butter can be made using the zest and a squeeze of juice from a citrus fruit: orange, lemon and lime are all good. Season with salt and pepper.

   Citrus butters can also be spiced up in other ways. Try lemon with a few blanched mint leaves, lime with some mustard, orange with a sprinkling of cinnamon or, even better, Seville orange with a little tomato purée and, if you like it, a touch of cayenne pepper.

# Watercress and Almond Butter

A lovely combination. Use ground almonds, or if you have a food processor, whole blanched almonds. Whole almonds always taste fresher and a food processor makes light work of grinding them.

SMALL BUNCH WATERCRESS
125g/4oz UNSALTED BUTTER
50g/2oz ALMONDS
LEMON JUICE
SALT AND PEPPER

Pick over the watercress then blanch, dry and chop it. Combine everything and season to taste.

# Anchovy Butter

4 ANCHOVY FILLETS, CHOPPED
50g/2oz UNSALTED BUTTER
PEPPER

Finely chop the anchovies, and using a wooden spoon beat them into the softened butter. Season with a little pepper.

# Mustard Butter

2 tbsp DIJON MUSTARD
½ tsp LEMON JUICE
50g/2oz BUTTER
SALT AND PEPPER

Amalgamate the mustard and lemon juice with the butter and season to taste.

# Paprika Butter

1 tsp LEMON JUICE
1 tsp PAPRIKA
50g/2oz BUTTER
SALT AND PEPPER

Mix the lemon juice into the paprika and then incorporate the paste into the butter. Season to taste.

# Montpellier Butter

I am intrigued by the fact that this salmon butter comes from a Mediterranean town. I can only conclude that a supply of salmon, having been caught in the Pyrennean rivers, used to find its way to the Montpellier market.

The inclusion of olive oil betrays the southern origins of this accompaniment, and I have seen recipes where the butter is omitted altogether. The balance between butter and oil varies and is usually at the discretion of the cook.

It is normally spread over cold, skinned salmon, but it can also be treated as the other butters and put in pats on to hot salmon.

125g/4oz MIXED HERBS: TARRAGON, CHERVIL, CHIVES, SPINACH, PARSLEY,
WATERCRESS (IF YOU CANNOT FIND CHERVIL INCREASE THE PARSLEY)
2 ANCHOVY FILLETS
1 GHERKIN
3 or 4 CAPERS
125g/4oz BUTTER
3 HARDBOILED EGG YOLKS
5 tbsp OLIVE OIL
GRATED NUTMEG
LEMON JUICE
SALT AND PEPPER

In a food processor finely chop the herbs, the anchovy fillets, the gherkin and the capers, then add the butter and the egg yolks. With the machine working, trickle in the oil through the feed tube. Season to taste with a little grated nutmeg, a squeeze of lemon juice and salt and pepper.

# Hollandaise Sauce

Hollandaise, delicious, unctuous and subtle, is *the* salmon sauce and the almost perfect accompaniment to a poached or steamed salmon cutlet or a piece of fillet.

Hollandaise can be made in the traditional way in a bowl standing over a pan of hot water, and I like to start it off by whisking a little cold butter into the egg yolks. This is a trick given by Margaret Costa in her *Four Seasons Cookbook* and does, I find, make it easier to obtain a lovely thick sauce. Otherwise Hollandaise can be made quickly, and with little danger of curdling, in a food processor or blender. The purists would say that the finished food processor version lacks some of the creaminess, but there is not much difference; and being almost foolproof it avoids the danger of turning into scrambled egg. I give instructions for both versions.

Clarified butter is not essential for a Hollandaise, but it does simplify the sauce making, and if you plan to hold the sauce over warm water, it is less likely to separate. To clarify butter, melt it slowly, skimming off any froth that rises to the surface. Leave it to stand for a minute, then pour the butter into a jug, stopping when you reach the milky sediment at the bottom of the pan. Discard the sediment, wash and dry the pan, return the butter to it and keep just warm.

Hollandaise is served warm or tepid, but once made it is not advisable to reheat it.

# *Traditional Hollandaise*

3 EGG YOLKS<br>
1 tbsp LEMON JUICE<br>
2 tbsp WATER<br>
SALT AND PEPPER<br>
25g/1oz COLD BUTTER<br>
175g/6oz WARM UNSALTED BUTTER (CLARIFIED, OPTIONAL)

Put the egg yolks, lemon juice, water and seasonings into a bowl and whisk them together. Place the bowl over a pan of hot, just shivering water, but do not let the base of the bowl heat up too much or touch the water. Whisk, adding the cold butter in small pieces, until the yolks have thickened and the butter has been incorporated. Then, spoonful by spoonful, whisk in the warm butter. If it shows any sign of separating, immediately remove the bowl from the heat and, whisking hard, either plunge the bottom into a bowl of cold water or add an ice cube, removing it when the sauce has stabilized again. If you cannot retrieve the sauce, start again and gradually whisk in the curdled mixture.

After the addition of all the butter, the sauce should be light and creamy. Finally, adjust the seasonings and, if liked, add a little more lemon juice.

The sauce can be kept over the cooling pan of hot water for about half an hour, but will separate if it is reheated.

# Food Processor or Blender Hollandaise

175g/6oz UNSALTED BUTTER
2 tbsp WATER
1 tbsp LEMON JUICE
3 EGG YOLKS
SALT AND PEPPER

Follow the instructions above for clarifying the butter, and after returning the butter to the pan, heat it to boiling point. At the same time, heat the water and lemon juice to boiling point, in another pan.

Put the egg yolks, salt and pepper into your blender or food processor and start the machine. After about 10 seconds add, through the lid, the boiling lemon and water and then the butter in a steady stream. Stop the machine when the sauce has thickened and amalgamated, check the seasoning and use as required.

# Ginger Hollandaise

Ginger and the flavourings in the following variations all add a 'zing' to a Hollandaise, but don't overdo the amount you add; the taste should just lurk in the background, leaving the sauce itself dominant.

Take about 2.5cm/1 inch fresh ginger, peel it and cut out any tough centre or core. Cut the remainder into thin matchsticks and put them in a pan with 2 tbsp white wine and 1 tbsp water. Heat and leave gently cooking until the ginger is tender, then, if necessary, increase the heat and reduce the liquid to around 1 tbsp.

If you are making the sauce by hand, add the ginger and liquid to the lemon juice and egg yolks just before you start whisking them. If by machine, strain off the liquid and heat it with the lemon juice. Add the ginger strips just before the machine is turned off, so that they are mixed in, but not puréed.

# Fennel Hollandaise

This is made in exactly the same way as Ginger Hollandaise, using about half of the heart of a small fennel bulb instead of the ginger.

# Mustard Hollandaise

Stir a couple of teaspoons of Dijon mustard into the finished sauce.

# Saffron Hollandaise

Steep ½tsp saffron shreds in 2 tbsp very hot water for 5 minutes, then stir it into the finished sauce.

# Maltaise Sauce

This should be made with blood oranges, which are usually available only in the early spring. If you can't get a blood orange, you might miss out a little on the colour, but you can use a sweet orange with a squeeze of lemon juice to sharpen it up.

Peel the zest from an orange, cut it into strips, blanch it in boiling water for 2 minutes, and then drain. Squeeze the juice from the orange and stir it, and the peel, into the sauce. Taste as you go, you may not need to use it all.

## Mousseline Sauce

Add 150ml/5 fl oz whipped double cream to a freshly made and warm Hollandaise. If necessary, dilute it with a little more lemon juice.

## Caviar Mousseline Sauce

This has an interesting texture, and if you are lucky enough to win the pools, it would be a truly magnificent experience to make it with the proper Beluga.

Make a Mousseline sauce and, just before serving, fold in the contents of a jar of lump-fish caviar.

Another extravagant, and nowadays almost impossible idea, but one that occurs frequently in 1930s cookery books, is to stir the coral of a lobster into the warm sauce.

## Béarnaise Sauce

Béarnaise and Hollandaise run in tandem and are made in much the same way. However, Hollandaise is very light and delicate, while Béarnaise is robust and much stronger. The two are often interchangeable, but I like to serve Hollandaise with hot poached salmon and Béarnaise, even if the sauce is warm, when the fish is at room temperature. Béarnaise is traditionally flavoured with tarragon, but I give other variations.

Like Hollandaise, Béarnaise can be made in the conventional way in a bain-marie, or quickly in a food processor or blender. I give both methods.

The sauce probably has its origins in southwest France or the Béarnais, but it is first recorded in about 1830 when it was made by the chef at the Pavillon Henri IV, at St Germain just outside Paris. The name is derived from the fact that Béarn was Henri IV's birthplace.

# Traditional Béarnaise

175g/6oz UNSALTED BUTTER
1 SHALLOT, FINELY CHOPPED
2 tbsp TARRAGON VINEGAR
150 ml/5 fl oz WHITE WINE
4-6 PEPPERCORNS, CRUSHED
3 EGG YOLKS
SALT

*To finish*
2 tbsp CHOPPED TARRAGON
1 tbsp CHOPPED CHERVIL OR PARSLEY

Clarify the butter (see page 44), and keep warm.

Finely chop the shallot and put it, together with the vinegar, white wine and pepper-corns, into a small heavy pan. Bring to the boil and cook gently until the liquid is re-duced to about 1 tbsp. Remove from the heat and stir in 2 tbsp cold water.

Put the egg yolks and salt into a bowl, whisk them together, and place the bowl over a pan of hot water. Strain in the white wine reduction, pressing hard with a wooden spoon to procure every drop. Continue whisking and adding the warm clarified butter in the same way as for Hollandaise (page 44).

When the butter has all been added and the sauce has thickened, stir in the chopped herbs and check the seasoning.

# Food Processor or Blender Béarnaise

Clarify the butter and keep it warm. Make the wine reduction in the same way as given above.

Put the egg yolks, salt and the reduction into your food processor or blender, start the motor, wait for the yolks and wine to amalgamate, then add the butter in a thin stream through the lid. When the sauce emulsifies, stop the machine. Before serving, correct the seasoning and stir in the herbs.

Chunky fish soup

## Béarnaise Sauce With Yoghurt

The finished sauce can be lightened by stirring in a few tablespoons of thick plain yoghurt.

## Béarnaise with Sorrel or Spinach

When you add another flavour to the sauce, it is best not to muddle it up with tarragon and to make the sauce using plain white wine vinegar.

Sorrel adds a marvellous, slightly acid bite and can now sometimes be found along with the packets of fresh herbs on the supermarket shelf. Otherwise, or as a change, use tender young spinach leaves; the taste will be different and somewhat milder.

You will need a handful of sorrel or spinach. Take a few leaves at a time, roll them up into a cigar and then cut across it to make little strips. Stir the strips into the hot newly made sauce and adjust the seasoning.

## Sauce Choron

Add 3-4 tsp tomato purée to the finished sauce.

## Béarnaise with Green Peppercorns

Stir about 1 tbsp green peppercorns into the sauce.

Pasta, artichoke and salmon salad

# Beurre Blanc

There is a story that beurre blanc came about because, somewhere around the turn of the century, the Marquis de Goulaine's cook, Clémence, forgot to include the eggs while making a Béarnaise sauce to accompany a pike. The success of the sauce enabled Clémence to open a restaurant near her home town of Nantes and this is where Mère Michel, who became famous for serving the sauce at her restaurant in Paris, first learnt how to make it. Incidentally the restaurant, near the Arc de Triomphe, still exists and still specializes in beurre blanc.

Whatever its origins, beurre blanc was *the* sauce of nouvelle cuisine; the imagination of the chefs brought out its versatility and it took its place alongside the other two classic hot emulsified sauces, Hollandaise and Béarnaise. It is rich, but not much is needed, and it adds a wonderful final touch to poached or grilled salmon or to a terrine or mousseline.

The sauce is quick to make and the reduction can be done ahead, but once made it will not hold for more than about 15 minutes and, if it should separate, it cannot be re-emulsified. The addition of a tablespoonful of cream to the wine reduction helps to stabilize the sauce and makes it less likely to separate, but it does mean that some of the buttery flavour is lost.

2 SHALLOTS, FINELY CHOPPED
4 tbsp DRY WHITE WINE
4 tbsp WHITE WINE VINEGAR
1 tbsp DOUBLE CREAM (OPTIONAL)
250g/8oz VERY COLD BUTTER
SALT AND PEPPER

Put the shallots, wine and vinegar in a small heavy bottomed pan. Bring to the boil, let it simmer gently and reduce to about 1 tbsp. Strain it, pushing with a wooden spoon to obtain all the liquid clinging to the shallots. Return the liquid to the pan. If you are using it, add the cream, bring back to the boil and reduce by half.

Cut the butter into cubes and, over a gentle heat, whisk them, one by one, into the sauce. If the emulsion shows any sign of overheating, remove the pan briefly from the heat and if necessary, cool it quickly by plunging the bottom into a bowl of cold water. When all the butter has been incorporated and the sauce is thick and glossy, set the sauce by turning up the heat and whisking constantly, bringing it to boiling point. Immediately it boils remove the pan from the heat. Season to taste and serve hot or warm.

# Beurre Blanc with Herbs

Stir 2 tbsp blanched chopped herbs into the finished sauce. Tarragon, dill and chervil are all good.

# Beurre Rose

A pink sauce for a pink fish, and one to make when you feel slightly flippant. In fact, its delicate sweetness marries well with salmon.

Make a beurre blanc using a rosé wine and raspberry vinegar, and just before serving it stir in about 1tsp crushed pink peppercorns.

# Béchamel Sauce

The ever useful classic sauce. It is often well worth while taking the time and trouble to infuse and flavour the milk, but don't bother if you need just a small amount of white sauce to mix with other strong flavours.

300ml/½ PINT MILK
½ SMALL ONION, CHOPPED
1 BAYLEAF, CRUMBLED
2 PARSLEY STALKS
6 BLACK PEPPERCORNS
25g/1oz BUTTER
25g/1oz FLOUR
SALT

Put the milk in a pan, add the onion, herbs and peppercorns and bring to the boil. Take the pan from the heat, cover it, leave to infuse for about half an hour and then strain and keep the milk.

In another pan melt the butter, sprinkle in the flour, and cook gently, stirring, for 1 minute.

Take the pan from the heat and, stirring all the time, add the strained milk. Return the pan to the hob and, still stirring, bring the sauce to the boil. Add salt to taste and simmer for a few minutes before using.

# Velouté

A velouté is made in the same way as a béchamel, but fish stock, or the court bouillon used for poaching the fish, is used to replace half, or frequently all, of the milk; the exact proportions are the choice of the cook. The sauce is lighter than a béchamel, and although it can be served just as it is, it is inclined to be a little thin in both consistency and taste. The French overcome the problem by enriching the velouté with egg yolks and cream, but another way of giving the sauce a shot in the arm is to cook the fish in foil with wine and butter, and to stir the juices from the packet into it.

In fish cookery a velouté often takes over the role normally played by a béchamel, as its lightness and flavour give it many advantages when making fish sauces or soups (see page 72). I give one or two ideas for flavouring it, but like any of the other basic sauces in the book, it is good with herbs, strips of sorrel, or some chopped cooked spinach.

40g/1½oz BUTTER
40g/1½oz FLOUR
600ml/1 pint FISH STOCK, OR MIXED MILK AND STOCK
SALT AND PEPPER

Melt the butter, stir in the flour and cook for a minute or so. Remove the pan from the heat and slowly stir in a few tablespoons of stock. When you have a smooth paste, return the pan to the heat, and stirring constantly, slowly add the remaining stock. Bring to the boil and let it simmer for 5 minutes, or a little longer if you wish to thicken and reduce the sauce further. Season with salt and pepper.

You can enrich the sauce by beating one or two egg yolks into a few tablespoons of cream and whisking it into the velouté.

## Tomato Velouté

Mix together 3-4 tbsp tomato purée and 150ml/5 fl oz single cream, and stir it into the hot velouté.

# Mustard Velouté

Mix together 3 tsp Dijon mustard and 3 tsp lemon juice and, tasting as you go, since you may not need it all, stir it into the velouté.

# Caper Sauce

A great favourite of mine.

Add 2 tbsp capers, 1 tsp wine vinegar and 2 tbsp chopped parsley to the velouté.

# Cucumber and Watercress Sauce

If you are serving salmon with plain boiled or steamed potatoes, the watercress in this sauce adds a nice peppery sting.

½ CUCUMBER
25g/1oz BUTTER
1 BUNCH WATERCRESS
300ml/½ PINT BÉCHAMEL SAUCE (PAGE 51)
1 tsp DIJON MUSTARD
2 tbsp THICK PLAIN YOGHURT

Peel the cucumber, split it in half lengthwise, cut out all the seeds and roughly chop it. In a small pan melt the butter. Add the cucumber and watercress and stir well. Put on a lid and cook over a low heat for about 20 minutes, or until the cucumber is soft and cooked.

Strain off any liquid and purée the cucumber and watercress in a food processor. Add the béchamel and the mustard and process for a few seconds to mix. Return the mixture to the saucepan, check the seasoning and reheat gently, stirring.

Just before serving the sauce take the pan from the heat and stir in the yoghurt.

# Egg Sauce

A good plain British sauce, but none the worse for that.

300ml/½ pint BÉCHAMEL (SEE PAGE 51)
½ BUNCH WATERCRESS
2 HARDBOILED EGGS, CHOPPED
1-2 tsp HORSERADISH SAUCE
SALT AND PEPPER

Pick over the watercress and discard the stalks. Chop the leaves and stir them and the eggs into a newly made béchamel sauce. Add horseradish sauce to taste, adjust the seasoning and add some extra milk if the sauce is too thick. Serve hot.

# Sauce Bâtarde

Sauce bâtarde or, to translate, bastard sauce, is sometimes known in English as mock Hollandaise. It is not as good as a proper Hollandaise, but it is nothing like as rich and is much easier to make.

300ml/½ pint LIGHT, SALTED FISH OR VEGETABLE STOCK
OR SALTED WATER
75-125g/3-4oz BUTTER
25g/1oz FLOUR
1 EGG YOLK
1 tbsp LEMON JUICE
PEPPER

Bring the stock or water to boiling point. In a separate pan melt 25g/1oz of the butter, stir in the flour and cook briefly. Pour in the boiling stock or water and, to avoid lumps forming, stir vigorously.

Whisk 1 tbsp cold water into the egg yolk and stir in a little of the hot sauce. Take the pan from the heat, whisk in the egg mixture, then return it and, stirring all the time, bring it up to boiling point.

Season to taste with pepper and lemon juice and once again, take the pan from the heat. Cut the remaining butter into dice and beat them one at a time into the sauce.

Serve the sauce immediately all the butter has been incorporated and it is smooth. This sauce will separate if reheated.

# Sauce Ravigote

I was fascinated to discover that *ravigoter* means 'to cheer up', and that is exactly what this is – a bucked-up version of sauce bâtarde.

2 SHALLOTS, FINELY CHOPPED
2 tbsp WHITE WINE VINEGAR
1 tsp EACH CHOPPED PARSLEY, CHIVES AND TARRAGON
½ tsp DIJON MUSTARD
300ml/½ pint SAUCE BÂTARDE (PAGE 54)

Put the shallots and vinegar in a small pan, heat gently and reduce by half. Strain, and stir the vinegar, herbs and mustard into the sauce.

# Sauce aux Câpres

Another way of bucking up the bastard!
    To 300 ml/½ pint sauce bâtarde add 2 tbsp capers, 1 tbsp chopped parsley and, if liked, a few drops of vinegar.

# Lemon Sauce

This sauce is one of my favourites. It is good either intensely lemony or milder and spiked with a cardamom. The addition of butter, which will slightly enrich the sauce and give it a nice gloss, is optional.

If you wish to make the sauce in advance, allow it to cool before you add the butter, stirring at intervals to stop a skin forming. It can then be refrigerated and kept for up to 24 hours.

1 tbsp CORNFLOUR
250ml/8fl oz FISH OR LIGHT VEGETABLE STOCK
JUICE OF 1-2 LEMONS
2 EGG YOLKS
½ tsp SUGAR
SALT AND PEPPER
25g/1oz BUTTER (OPTIONAL)

Slake the cornflour by stirring in a couple of tablespoons of the stock.

In a pan combine the stock and lemon juice. Whisk in the egg yolks, the cornflour mixture, the sugar, and salt and pepper to taste. Slowly heat the pan, stirring all the time, until it reaches boiling point and the sauce thickens.

If you are using butter whisk it into the sauce just before you serve it.

# Lemon Sauce with cardamom

4-5 CARDAMOM PODS
275ml/9fl oz FISH OR LIGHT VEGETABLE STOCK
1 tbsp CORNFLOUR
JUICE OF 1 LEMON
2 EGG YOLKS
½ tsp SUGAR
SALT AND PEPPER
25g/1oz BUTTER (OPTIONAL)

Remove the seeds from the cardamom pods and crush them to a powder in a pestle and mortar, or with a small hammer on a chopping board. Add the crushed seeds to the stock and make the sauce in the same way as the Lemon sauce above.

# Mayonnaise

The first rule with mayonnaise, unless you are mixing a small quantity into other ingredients, is to forget about the jars and make it yourself. People are, I think, frightened of making mayonnaise, but it isn't difficult and it is very satisfying to watch the emulsion form and hold together.

Mayonnaise making is much eased if you have all the ingredients at room temperature; you will then find that the oil immediately starts to blend into the egg yolk, and once an emulsion has been established, you should have no further problems. If it should separate, you can always bring it back by using another egg yolk and slowly whisking the curdled mixture into it.

You can flavour and thin the mayonnaise with either vinegar or lemon juice, and if you decide on lemon juice, start with only a teaspoon or so as it is a powerful thinner. Mustard acts as a stabilizer and helps to start the emulsion off, but if you find it gives too strong a flavour, leave it out.

The oil you use is a matter of preference, but choose one that will blend with the food you propose serving. Sunflower oil makes a perfectly good mayonnaise, and being bland is perhaps the one to use if you plan to add other ingredients or flavours. I find that mayonnaise made with olive oil is very heavy, but to retain its flavour, I often leave out the mustard and use a mixture of one part olive oil to two parts sunflower. I do the same with a nut oil, reducing the proportions of the strong oil even more.

The quantities given should make a glossy mayonnaise with a consistency that will hold peaks. If you want to use it as a coating sauce, dilute it by stirring in a spoonful or two of warm water.

Like many other sauces, mayonnaise can be flavoured with herbs or other ingredients, and the variations I give are especially suitable for a mayonnaise that is going to be served with cold salmon. For a party you can serve a variety: a plain one and two others with different colours and flavours.

2 EGG YOLKS
2 tbsp WINE VINEGAR OR 1 tbsp LEMON JUICE
1 tsp MUSTARD (OPTIONAL)
300ml/½ pint OIL
SALT AND PEPPER

Whisk together the egg yolks, half the vinegar or lemon juice and, if using it, the mustard. Drip in the oil, making sure that each drop is whisked into the mixture before adding the next. When you have used about a third of the oil and an emulsion has formed, you can start dribbling it in more quickly. Finally, after all the oil has been incorporated, stir in enough vinegar or lemon juice to achieve the right consistency and season with salt and pepper.

# Food Processor Mayonnaise

Mayonnaise can be made very quickly in a food processor. Process together the egg yolks, vinegar or lemon juice and mustard and then, with the machine running, add the oil through the feed tube. Start with a very slow trickle and then, once an emulsion has been formed, increase it to a steady stream. Food processor mayonnaise can become heavy, so make it as quickly as you can and stop the machine immediately all the oil has been added.

# Light Mayonnaise

Mayonnaise, which is too rich for some people's taste, can easily be lightened, and some would say the taste improved, by stirring in 2-3 tbsp yoghurt. Serve as it is, or flavour it further.

# Sauce Verte

Use about 125g/4oz mixed leaves and herbs. Include some, and if possible all, of the following: spinach, watercress, tarragon and parsley. Blanch them, squeeze dry, chop and stir into the mayonnaise. Or use a food processor and purée them into the mayonnaise.

If you like a stronger taste, you can also add a little finely chopped shallot or garlic.

# Tomato mayonnaise

Stir 1-2 tbsp tomato purée into the mayonnaise.

# Fennel Mayonnaise

Use half a fennel bulb, trim off the feathery fronds and any tough outside leaves, cut in half again and cook, in boiling salted water, until tender. Purée in a food processor or blender and stir into the mayonnaise.

# Avocado Mayonnaise

Mash or purée half a ripe avocado, stir it into the mayonnaise and season, if liked, with a pinch of cayenne pepper.

# Anchovy Mayonnaise

Anchovies add a distinctive flavour to mayonnaise. Make a basic mayonnaise but don't add any salt. Mash 2-4 anchovy fillets and stir, or process, them in.

# Campari and Orange Mayonnaise

I tried out this unusual mayonnaise on some friends; they ate it all and made me promise to include it here.

Make a mayonnaise replacing the lemon or vinegar with orange juice. Stir in the zest of the orange and, tasting as you go, up to 1 tbsp Campari.

# Sauce Gribiche

A cold sauce, based like mayonnaise on egg yolk, but cooked rather than raw. When serving this sauce I like to decorate the salmon with more hardboiled eggs, some cucumber, baby tomatoes and a few black olives.

2 HARDBOILED EGGS
300 ml/½ PINT OIL
2 tbsp WHITE WINE VINEGAR
2 tbsp FINELY CHOPPED GHERKIN
1 tbsp CAPERS
2 tbsp CHOPPED PARSLEY
ZEST OF ½ LEMON

Separate the yolks from the whites of the eggs, chop the whites and keep on one side. Mash the yolks and gradually, beating all the time, add the oil. When the mixture is thick and smooth, stir in all the remaining ingredients and season to taste.

# Martini Rosso Sauce

A real treat – dish it up with cold salmon. The red vermouth and the sharp vinegar are a great antithesis and make a lovely sauce. I have adapted this from a recipe for vermouth sauce that I found in *Vogue's French Cookery Book*, published in 1961. I have altered it little except for substituting balsamic vinegar for shallot-flavoured vinegar.

2 tbsp ITALIAN RED VERMOUTH
2 tsp BALSAMIC VINEGAR
1 tsp PAPRIKA
½ tsp DIJON MUSTARD
PINCH CAYENNE PEPPER
SALT AND EPPPER
150ml/¼ pint DOUBLE CREAM

Leaving out the cream, mix together all the ingredients. Add the cream and whisk it, or process it in a food processor, until it thickens. Refrigerate until needed.

# Walnut and Horseradish Sauce

Elizabeth David in *French Provincial Cooking* quotes Escoffier's description of a shooting weekend in the Haute-Savoie sometime early this century. For lunch on Sunday they had a local lake fish (salmon trout) accompanied by 'a completely original sauce', for which he gives the recipe.

Elizabeth David gives her version of the sauce saying: 'I have come to the conclusion that it is an even better sauce for this lovely and delicate fish than the more usual sauce verte.'

I am inclined to agree, and my version is little altered from her own, except that I use a food processor to chop the nuts, and, as fresh horseradish is seldom available, a good quality jar of hot creamed horseradish.

75g/3oz SHELLED WALNUTS
2-3 tbsp HOT HORSERADISH CREAM
150ml/¼ pint DOUBLE CREAM
SALT
LEMON JUICE
SUGAR (OPTIONAL)

As Elizabeth David says, this is a very much finer sauce when made with skinned walnuts. They are tedious to skin, but the amount needed is not enormous; it is easiest to do them in batches. Bring a pan of water to simmering point, add a few walnuts, leave for two minutes, and then use a slotted spoon to take them out. While they are still hot, and using a sharp pointed knife, scrape off the skin.

Using a blender or food processor chop the nuts, then mix them with 2 tbsp horseradish and the cream. Season to taste with salt and lemon juice and possibly a little sugar. Check again, and if you want more 'bite', stir in a further spoonful of horseradish.

# Watercress Sauce

You can use double cream to make a really unctuous sauce or, for something less rich, dilute it with yoghurt or crème fraîche. The proportions are up to you, but to retain a smoothness in the sauce I would use at least 25ml/1fl oz cream.

Serve the sauce, hot, warm or cold, at the most suitable temperature for the food.

LARGE HANDFUL WATERCRESS LEAVES
150ml/¼ pint DOUBLE CREAM, OR CREAM AND YOGHURT OR CRÈME FRAÎCHE
SALT AND PEPPER

Plunge the leaves into a pan of boiling water and after 30 seconds drain and refresh under a cold tap. Put the leaves and cream, or cream and yoghurt, into a food processor and process to purée the watercress. Pour into a pan and, stirring, bring it to the boil, then remove from the heat and, if you wish, strain it. Season and keep covered until needed.

# Avocado Sauce

This is based on Mexican guacamole. The amount of chilli used depends on whether you like it mild or spicy.

1-2 SPRING ONIONS
1 AVOCADO
2 tbsp LEMON OR LIME JUICE
¼ tsp CORIANDER SEEDS, CRUSHED
SMALL PINCH CHILLI POWDER
1 tbsp TOMATO PURÉE
150ml/¼ pint FROMAGE FRAIS OR YOGHURT
SALT AND PEPPER

Trim the spring onion or onions, discard the green part, chop the rest and put into the bowl of a food processor. Halve the avocado, discard the stone and spoon in the flesh. Add the lemon or lime juice, spices and tomato purée and process until smooth. Spoon in the fromage frais or yoghurt, season and process to mix. Transfer to a bowl and use within an hour or so, or the avocado will discolour.

# Light Herb Sauce

A simple quick sauce that can be flavoured with any herb, but with salmon I would use either dill or tarragon. If you like it mild you can leave out the shallot.

150ml/¼ pint SOURED CREAM
1 tbsp CHOPPED DILL OR TARRAGON
1 tsp FINELY CHOPPED SHALLOT
SALT AND PEPPER

Mix the cream, herb and shallot together and season with salt and pepper.

# Red Pepper Sauce

A light low-fat sauce. If you want to eat it with hot salmon heat the puréed pepper and add the yoghurt after taking it from the heat.

1 RED PEPPER
1 tbsp TOMATO PURÉE
1 tsp PAPRIKA
150ml/¼ pint YOGHURT
SALT AND PEPPER

Cut the pepper into quarters and cut out and throw away the stalk, seeds and any inner membrane. Grill, skin side upwards, until the skin is black and charred. Leave to cool, then peel off the skin.

Roughly chop the skinned quarters, put them in a blender or food processor and process with the tomato purée until they are puréed. Turn into a bowl, stir in the paprika, and if eating the sauce cold, the yoghurt. Finally, season to taste.

# Samphire Sauce

A small amount of samphire can be made into an attractive sauce to serve with hot salmon. Take about 50g/2oz picked-over samphire tops, chop finely and stir into 150ml/¼ pint double cream or crème fraîche. Transfer to a saucepan, bring to the boil and cook until the samphire is tender and the liquid has reduced to the consistency of a sauce. Grind on some black pepper and taste to see if salt is needed. If you want a smooth sauce, whizz it all up in a food processor, otherwise use as it is.

# Fresh Tomato Coulis

A summer sauce and one that needs to be made with well flavoured tomatoes. Like all tomato sauces its uses are legion: one way I like to serve it is spooned over a piece of freshly cooked salmon surrounded by a few whirls of lightly buttered glistening tagliatelle.

If you like a smoother and less intense sauce you can stir in some cream or soured cream.

500g/1lb RIPE SWEET TOMATOES
50g/2oz BUTTER
SALT, PEPPER AND SUGAR
1 BUNCH FRESH BASIL

Peel the tomatoes then cut each one in half and discard the seeds and any hard stalk or core. Roughly chop the remaining tomato flesh. In a small frying pan melt the butter, add the tomatoes and season with salt, pepper and a little sugar. Cook, stirring constantly, over a low heat. The moment the tomatoes are hot, take the pan from the heat.

The coulis also cooks well in a microwave. Put the chopped tomatoes, butter and seasonings into a dish. Cover leaving an air hole, or stretch a piece of clingfilm over the dish and pierce it with a knife once or twice. Microwave on high for 1 minute, take from the oven, stir well and correct the seasonings.

Just before serving the coulis sprinkle it liberally with shredded basil.

# Warm Tomato Dressing

This dressing is based on one for red mullet in Richard Stein's *English Seafood Cookery*. It is an alternative to the tomato coulis: that is based on butter and this on a good fruity olive oil. Use the sauce that is most appropriate to the way you have cooked the salmon or to its accompaniments.

500g/1lb TOMATOES, PEELED, DESEEDED AND CHOPPED
1 tsp CHOPPED HERBS: PARSLEY, TARRAGON, DILL OR BASIL
1 SHALLOT, FINELY CHOPPED
75ml/3fl oz OLIVE OIL
JUICE OF ½ LEMON
SALT AND PEPPER

In a small saucepan mix all the ingredients together and warm through; don't let the tomatoes cook or get too hot.

# Barbecue Sauce

This strong flavoured sauce is best with char-grilled salmon (page 34), but if it should rain, and you have to come into the kitchen and put the fish under the grill, don't worry; the sauce will still taste good.

1-2 CLOVES GARLIC
SPRIG MINT
1 tsp DIJON MUSTARD
1 tbsp TOMATO PURÉE
1 tbsp WHITE WINE VINEGAR
1 tsp SUGAR
SALT AND PEPPER
150ml/¼ pint SUNFLOWER OIL

Crush the garlic, finely chop the mint and, either in a bowl or a food processor, mix in all the other ingredients except for the oil. When they are amalgamated add the oil. Check the seasoning and use as required.

# Cucumber Salad

The simplest of salads is made by sprinkling paper-thin cucumber slices with a little sweet vinaigrette sauce, mixing well and leaving for an hour or so. Just before serving the salad, drain off most of the liquid and sprinkle the cucumber with parsley or dill.

# Yoghurt and Cucumber Salad

This is a version of Greek tzatziki.

Peel a cucumber, slice or shred it and leave it, sprinkled with salt, to drain for about half an hour. Use kitchen paper to pat off any excess moisture and then mix the cucumber with 300ml/½ pint yoghurt, a few chopped mint leaves and seasonings.

You can replace the yoghurt with soured cream, crème fraîche, or a mixture of any of them.

# Salad Elona

Who Elona was I do not know, but Jane Grigson, among others, seems to have discovered her and she gave her name to a very attractive salad.

Interleave equal amounts of sliced cucumber and sliced strawberries on a plate, give a good grinding of pepper, sprinkle with salt and sugar and pour over a little dry white wine or wine vinegar.

I tried substituting kiwi fruit for the strawberries and it worked perfectly, giving a cool looking and very decorative salad.

Alternatively, and it would look very pretty, you could decorate a whole fish by interleaving the cucumber 'scales' with either strawberries or kiwi fruit.

# Cucumber mould

This is slightly more substantial than the previous salad, but it goes well alongside plain cold salmon and a green salad. It can also be made a day ahead and kept in the refrigerator. Serves 6-8.

300ml/½ pint LIGHT CHICKEN OR VEGETABLE STOCK
3 tsp/1 PACKET GELATINE
125g/4oz CREAM CHEESE OR CURD CHEESE
2 tbsp WHITE WINE VINEGAR
1 tbsp SUGAR
SALT AND PEPPER
1 CUCUMBER
LEAVES FROM 1 BUNCH WATERCRESS OR PUNNET MUSTARD AND CRESS
2-3 SPRING ONIONS, FINELY CHOPPED

Melt the gelatine in 2 tbsp stock, then add it to the remaining stock and, little by little, beat it into the cheese. Add the vinegar and sugar and season with salt and pepper. Leave on one side but don't let it set.

Peel the cucumber, cut it lengthwise into quarters and cut out and discard the seeds. Cut each quarter lengthwise into 2 or 3 and chop across to dice it.

When the stock and cheese mixture starts to thicken, stir in the cucumber, cress and onions and pour into an oiled mould. Cover and refrigerate until needed.

# SOUPS, FIRST COURSES
# AND SALADS

The first course should titillate the appetite and set the scene for what is to follow, and salmon, which can so easily be transformed into something that is both light and colourful, fits the bill perfectly.

These recipes are very mixed: some very light, some more substantial, and some equally suitable for lunch or a light main course. It is, as always, at the discretion of the cook.

The most common way of serving cold salmon is along with salads and mayonnaise but, on occasions, when there is salmon to be used up or fewer people to be catered for, it is nice to include the fish as part of the salad.

I give some suggestions on pages 92-95 and you can alter them according to your whim or the time of year. I like to use two or three different lettuces or coloured leaves and find the ready packed mixed salads from supermarkets very useful. For two or three people, they are much less extravagant than buying everything separately. Add other raw or blanched vegetables to the basic salad leaves: cucumber, a few radishes, baby courgettes, mangetouts, grilled and skinned peppers. It is up to you to mix and match and have fun with colours, shapes and textures.

## *Iced Yoghurt and Salmon Soup*

Perfect for a hot summer's day, cool, refreshing and quick: there's no need to drag yourself from the great outside and the comfort of a garden chair for more than a few minutes.

175g/6oz COOKED SALMON
600ml/1 pint WELL JELLIED CHICKEN STOCK, OR CANNED CHICKEN CONSOMMÉ
AND WATER TO MAKE 600ml/1 pint
300ml/½ pint YOGHURT
½ CUCUMBER
SALT AND PEPPER
4 tbsp CREAM

Flake the salmon and put it, and a little of the stock, into a blender or food processor and reduce to a purée.

Beat the yoghurt until smooth, then stir it, and the salmon mixture, into the stock. Refrigerate until needed.

Half an hour or so before you plan to eat, grate the cucumber, sprinkle it lightly with salt and put to drain in a sieve.

When you are ready, use a sheet of kitchen paper to pat any excess salt from the cucumber, then stir the cucumber into the soup. Taste, adjust the seasonings, ladle it into four bowls and finally dribble a swirl of cream into the centre of each.

# Avocado and Salmon Soup

I am never quite sure of the merits of hot avocado, but here it works, and adds a nice additional flavour to a warming winter soup. It can be made with either a fresh salmon steak or some leftover fish.

175g/6oz POTATO, PEELED AND CUBED
1 SMALL ONION, FINELY SLICED
1 CLOVE GARLIC, CRUSHED
25g/1oz BUTTER
1 AVOCADO PEAR
SMALL BUNCH DILL
SALT AND PEPPER
150-175g/5-6oz SALMON STEAK OR 125g/4oz COOKED SALMON, FLAKED
½ LEMON

In a saucepan melt the butter, put in the potato, onion and garlic then cover the pan and cook, giving it an occasional shake, for 5 minutes.

Roughly chop the avocado flesh and add it to the pan. Pour in 1.2 litres/2 pints water, add the stalks from the dill, season with salt and pepper and bring to simmering point.

If you are using uncooked salmon, put it into the pan and poach for 6-8 minutes or until just cooked. Then remove it and skin, bone and flake it.

Leave the pan to simmer for a further 10 minutes, or until the potato is very soft, then take it from the heat, strain off the stock and discard the dill stalks. Turn the contents of the strainer into a food processor or blender, add the salmon and a little of the stock and process until smooth.

Return the purée and the reserved liquid to the pan and stir to amalgamate. Squeeze in some lemon juice and correct the seasoning.

The soup will keep, covered and refirgerated, for a few hours. When needed, gently reheat it, then serve in warm bowls and sprinkle with chopped dill.

# Chunky Fish Soup

Substantial and filling, this should perhaps be called a stew rather than a soup. It is, I think, more appropriate for a main course, and a very satisfying meal can be achieved by serving a light first course and then following the soup with salad and cheese. For something less extravagant, you could substitute plaice and cod or haddock for the lemon sole and monkfish, but it would not be quite so good.

300-375g/10-12oz SALMON
1 LEMON SOLE
300g/10oz MONKFISH
50g/2oz BUTTER
1 SMALL ONION, CHOPPED
1 CLOVE GARLIC, CRUSHED
2 tbsp PAPRIKA
1 tsp DIJON OR SWEDISH GOURMET MUSTARD
400g/14oz CAN TOMATOES
FEW STALKS DILL
2 BAY LEAVES
300ml/½ pint DOUBLE CREAM
SALT AND PEPPER
125g/4oz PRAWNS

Fillet and skin the fish, or if you ask your fishmonger to do it, be sure to bring home the bones. Roll up the lemon sole fillets and secure them with a cocktail stick. Divide the other fish into chunks and then put the fish into a dish, cover it, and refrigerate until needed.

Make a fish stock. Put the bones into a saucepan with 900ml/1½ pints water, bring to the boil and simmer fast for 20 minutes, then drain off the stock. This can also be done in a microwave: place the bones and water in a large bowl, leaving lots of headroom or it will bubble out, cover with clingfilm, pierce once or twice with a knife, and microwave on high for 15 minutes.

In a large clean pan melt the butter and put in the onion and garlic. Stir, and when the onion starts to sizzle, sprinkle on the paprika. Cook for a minute, stir in the mustard and the can of tomatoes, then pour in the fish stock and add the dill (stalks only) and the bay leaves. Bring to the boil, cover and simmer gently for an hour. This can all be done ahead.

Strain off the liquid, discard the dill stalks and bay leaves, and blend, or process to a purée, the remaining contents of the sieve. Combine the purée with the liquid, stir in the cream and season with salt and pepper. Bring it all back to simmering point and poach the fish, adding it in order: first the monkfish, then, after 2 minutes, the salmon and, finally, after a further minute the lemon sole and prawns. Have ready four hot bowls and, a minute after the last addition, start retrieving the fish. Divide it, as evenly as you can, between the bowls, pour over the liquid, sprinkle with dill and serve with plenty of crusty bread and butter.

# Creamy Summer Soup

Vichyssoise, made with leeks, potatoes and cream, is the 'king' of cold soups and is good with some salmon flaked into it. However, in the summer decent leeks are hard to come by and this version, which is based on Hannah Wright's recipe for Crème Vichyssoise in her book *Soups*, very successfully substitutes shallots or spring onions for the leeks. As she says: 'It is an equally glamorous and delicious alternative.'

To bring out the salmon flavour and to give the soup an extra fillip I have spiced it with star anise, a very attractive looking Chinese seasoning and one that is now easily found in shop spice racks.

1 SMALLISH POTATO
3 SHALLOTS OR 5-10 SPRING ONIONS (DEPENDING ON THEIR SIZE)
450ml/¾ pint MILK
2 STAR ANISE
SALT AND PEPPER
1 LARGE (OR 2 SMALL) SALMON STEAKS OR 150-175g/5-6oz COLD SALMON
150g/5oz CREAM CHEESE OR COTTAGE CHEESE
50g/2oz PIECE OF UNPEELED CUCUMBER
½ PUNNET MUSTARD AND CRESS

Peel and slice the potato and the shallots or spring onions, using the white parts only. Discard the green tops or keep them for a salad or a more rustic soup. Put the vegetables into a saucepan, add the milk and the star anise and season lightly with salt and pepper. Bring to boiling point and, if using fresh salmon, poach it in the milk for 6-10 minutes, or until it is cooked, then remove and allow to cool. Keep refrigerated until needed.

Keep the milk at simmering point for around 20 minutes in total or until the potato is very soft. Take from the heat, strain off and keep the liquid. Discard the star anise. Put the vegetables into a blender or food processor, add the cream or cottage cheese and reduce it all to a purée. Amalgamate the purée with the reserved liquid, cover the bowl and allow to cool. Refrigerate until needed, but for no more than 24 hours.

An hour or so before you plan to eat, flake the salmon, coarsely grate the cucumber, and stir them into the soup with the mustard and cress. Leave in the fridge. Just before serving the soup, give it another stir, taste, and, if necessary, add further seasonings.

# Velouté of Salmon with Shrimps

A fish soup based on a velouté thickened and enriched with cream and egg yolks can be found on many menus, especially in France. The soup is rich and smooth; the inclusion of puréed salmon makes it a beguiling shade of pale peach and the shrimps add an extra delicacy to the flavour. If you like to restrict your fat consumption, you could make a simpler version by forgetting about the eggs and cream and using a little extra flour in the velouté.

250g/8oz SALMON
1.2 litres/2 pints FISH STOCK (SEE PAGE 37)
40g/1½oz BUTTER
40g/1½oz FLOUR
2 EGG YOLKS
150ml/¼ pint SINGLE CREAM
125g/4oz SHRIMPS
1-2 tbsp BRANDY
SALT AND PEPPER
CHOPPED DILL

Poach the salmon in half the fish stock. Skin and bone the cooked fish and keep it, and the stock, on one side.

Use the butter, flour and remaining stock to make a velouté (see page 00).

Flake the fish into a blender or food processor, pour in a little of the reserved stock, whizz it to a purée and pour it, and the remaining stock, into the velouté. Whisk the egg yolks and the cream together, pour them into the soup and heat gently, stirring all the time, until the soup has thickened. Bring it just to the boil and simmer, stirring frequently, for 2-3 minutes.

Take the pan from the heat, add the shrimps and a splash of brandy, and season to taste. Warm the shrimps by returning the pan briefly to a low heat, but do not let it boil. Serve immediately in heated bowls.

The soup will keep, covered and refrigerated, for a few hours. When needed, gently reheat, then pour it into warm bowls and sprinkle with chopped dill.

# Salmon and Tomato En Gelée

A light summery first course. Perhaps rather lazily, I have given instructions for making it with a packet of aspic jelly, but if you have some clear fish stock, use it, and add a little gelatine if necessary.

250g/8oz COOKED SALMON
375g/12oz TOMATOES
1 PACKET ASPIC JELLY
WINE VINEGAR
SMALL HANDFUL FRESH BASIL
A LITTLE OIL
SALT AND PEPPER

Follow the instructions to make the aspic jelly, and if you think it needs it, sharpen it up with a splash of vinegar. Let it cool and then keep it in a warm place so that it will not set. Lightly oil four ramekins and put them to chill in the fridge, or even better, in the freezing compartment.

Remove and reserve four leaves from the basil and finely chop the remainder. Peel the tomatoes, deseed them and chop the flesh into small pieces. Mix in a little salt and the chopped basil. Flake the salmon.

Pour a little aspic jelly into the bottom of each ramekin and put a basil leaf, with its top side downwards, on top of it. Return the ramekins to the fridge or freezer for a few minutes for the jelly to set.

When it has set, spoon in the tomatoes and pour over enough aspic jelly to just cover them. Put them back in the fridge or freezer.

When the tomato layer has set, cover it with the salmon, then fill the ramekins to the top with some more of the jelly, but don't worry if there is some left over. Leave them in the fridge until needed.

To serve, turn each one on to a plate and serve as it is, with another sprig of basil for decoration, or with some lettuce leaves and a small dollop of mayonnaise.

# Spinach and Salmon Soufflé

A soufflé is as basic to a cook in France as scrambled eggs are to a cook in Britain. The British have always been frightened of soufflés and think, wrongly, that they are difficult to make and impossible to time. There are two important rules, and as long as these are adhered to nobody should have any trouble. Firstly, use a proper soufflé dish with straight sides, and secondly at *le moment juste* make sure everybody is sitting down and waiting. Jane Grigson put it beautifully in *English Food*, when she said: 'In a properly trained household, the cry of "Soufflé!" should have the same effect of assembly as "Fire!".' If your cries do not work, you can hold the soufflé by turning the oven down to very low, keeping the door tight shut and leaving it for up to 10 minutes; but you may find that this treatment slightly dries it up.

This recipe is for a straightforward soufflé with chopped spinach and flaked, cooked salmon mixed into it. It is always difficult to know how much fresh spinach to buy, but 375-400g/12-14oz should produce around 125g/4oz after washing, picking over and cooking. Otherwise use about 250g/8oz frozen spinach.

300ml/½ pint MILK
½ SMALL ONION, ROUGHLY CHOPPED
1 BAYLEAF
6 PEPPERCORNS
½ CLOVE GARLIC (OPTIONAL)
50g/2oz BUTTER
40g/1½oz PLAIN FLOUR
4 EGG YOLKS
125g/4oz CHOPPED COOKED SPINACH
250g/8oz COOKED SALMON, FLAKED
5 EGG WHITES
SALT AND PEPPER

Put the milk, onion, bayleaf, peppercorns and, if using it, garlic into a saucepan and bring to just below boiling point. Remove it from the heat, cover and leave to infuse for 10-15 minutes or until needed.

In another saucepan, melt the butter, add the flour and cook gently, stirring frequently for 2-3 minutes. Strain in the warm milk, whisk until smooth and simmer for a minute or two. Remove the pan from the heat and, one at a time, add the egg yolks, then stir in the spinach and salmon. Season, cover tightly and leave until needed; if kept in a refrigerator this mixture can be made up to 24 hours in advance.

Generously butter the inside of a 1.4 litre/2½ pint soufflé dish. Heat the oven to 190°C/375°F/gas 5, and place a baking tray on the centre shelf.

If the soufflé mixture has been cooled and kept, reheat until it is hand hot. Whisk the egg whites with a pinch of salt until stiff, then stir a large spoonful into the mixture; this will relax and slacken it. Using a metal spoon or spatula and a light hand, fold the two mixtures together.

Spoon into the prepared dish, place on the baking tray in the oven, shut the door and leave to cook for 25-30 minutes, depending on how creamy you like the centre to be.

# Light Tarragon Flavoured Soufflé

I have experimented with several flourless soufflé mixtures and have come to the conclusion that this very simple one, based on a mousseline and without even one egg yolk, is the best. I found a plain version, to which I have added the crème fraîche and tarragon, in Anne Willan's *Real Food*, and she in turn gives credit for the recipe to Henri Babinski, known as Ali-Bab, who gave it in *Livre de Cuisine* in 1912.

As with any mousseline mixture you need to keep everything very cold, so before starting, chill the salmon, egg whites and cream in the freezer for 20 minutes and, if you have room, put your food processor bowl in as well.

The soufflé makes a lovely light first course. Serve it with the tarragon flavoured beurre blanc on page 51.

300g/10oz SALMON
4 EGG WHITES
A FEW TARRAGON LEAVES, CHOPPED
SALT AND PEPPER
150ml/¼ pint DOUBLE CREAM
75ml/3fl oz CRÈME FRAÎCHE

Generously grease a 900ml-1.2 litre/1½-2 pint soufflé dish. Preheat the oven to 180°C/350°F/gas 4, put a large dish or bain-marie into it and fill it with very hot water.

Whisk one egg white until it froths then add to it the tarragon and seasonings. Cut the salmon into pieces and purée it in a food processor for a minute or until it is completely smooth. Keep your machine running and slowly pour in the whisked egg white followed by the cream and the crème fraîche, and when the mixture thickens stop the machine. Briefly return the mixture to the fridge or freezing compartment.

Add a pinch of salt to the 3 remaining egg whites and whisk them until stiff. Stir a spoonful of egg white into the mousseline mixture and then carefully fold in the remainder. Spoon the mixture into the prepared dish and cook for 20-25 minutes, or until the centre is firm to the touch.

While it is cooking, make the tarragon flavoured beurre blanc. Hand it round separately or turn the soufflé out and pour the sauce over it.

# Swiss Soufflés

These soufflés are cooked, or rather poached, in individual ramekins in a bain-marie and then turned out on to artichoke bottoms, covered with a cream sauce, and returned to the oven until they are golden and bubbling. Serves 4 as main course, 6-8 as a first course. Beware that cans of artichoke bottoms do not always yield a round half dozen!

250g/8oz SALMON
25g/1oz BUTTER
25g/1oz FLOUR
125ml/4fl oz MILK
2 EGGS PLUS 2 WHITES
SALT AND PEPPER
300ml/½ pint CRÈME FRAÎCHE OR DOUBLE CREAM
25g/1oz BUTTER KNEADED WITH 15g/½oz FLOUR TO MAKE BEURRE MANIÉ
6 CANNED ARTICHOKE BOTTOMS

Generously grease four small soufflé dishes or six to eight ramekins.

Preheat the oven to 180°C/350°F/gas 4 and place in it a baking tray or dish large enough to hold the soufflé dishes. Fill the dish two-thirds full of water and leave it to heat up in the oven.

If necessary, skin and bone the salmon, then cut it into chunks. Put it into a food processor.

In a small saucepan melt the butter, stir in the flour and let it cook for a couple of minutes. Add the milk and stir over the heat until you have a very thick and smooth sauce.

Add the sauce to the salmon and process them together until the salmon is puréed. With the machine running add the whole eggs and season well with salt and pepper.

Add a pinch of salt to the whites and whisk them until stiff. Fold the salmon mixture into them and spoon into the prepared dishes.

Put the dishes in the hot water and cook for 20 minutes for small soufflés and 15 minutes for ramekins.

While the soufflés are cooking, stabilize the cream by warming it and stirring in the beurre manié bit by bit. Continue stirring the cream, without boiling, until it is thick and smooth, then remove the pan from the heat.

Generously grease an ovenproof dish large enough to hold the soufflés, and place the required number of artichoke bottoms in it.

When the soufflés are cooked, remove them from the oven and leave them to cool slightly. Run a knife or spatula round each one, unmould it into your hand then turn it back on to an artichoke bottom. Spoon the cream over the top and return to the oven for 10 minutes.

# Rillettes

Pork rillettes are to be found in every charcuterie in France and I have taken the name for this salmon pâté because it has the same texture and feel to it. I did try cutting out the butter and making it entirely with fromage frais, but when cooled it stayed sloppy and didn't taste nearly as good. Make it with a tailpiece or any uncooked leftovers of salmon and, if available, use smoked salmon trimmings.

Serve it as it is, with plenty of hot crusty bread or, even better, with toasted slices of an Italian bread such as focaccia as part of the Piatto Italiano on page 78.

175g/6oz SALMON, BONED AND SKINNED
50g/2oz SMOKED SALMON
1 SMALL CLOVE GARLIC
2 tbsp OLIVE OIL
2 OR 3 SPRIGS THYME
25g/1oz BUTTER
1 tsp BRANDY (OPTIONAL)
2 tbsp FROMAGE FRAIS OR GREEK YOGHURT
LEMON JUICE
SALT AND PEPPER

Peel the garlic clove and cut into 3 or 4 pieces. Pour the oil in a frying pan and add the garlic and thyme. Heat it very gently and let it just sizzle for about 10 minutes. Occasionally squash down the garlic and herbs with a wooden spoon, but do not let the garlic colour or it will leave a bitter taste. Meanwhile, cut the fresh salmon into cubes and the smoked salmon into matchstick pieces.

Remove the garlic and thyme from the pan, add the fresh salmon and stir constantly for a minute or two or until it is just cooked. Pour the contents of the pan into a food processor or blender.

Put the butter in the pan, melt it, add the smoked salmon, and the moment it starts to change colour, take the pan from the heat.

Add the brandy (if you are using it) and the fromage frais to the food processor or blender and process very briefly to just mix everything. Add the smoked salmon, a squeeze of lemon juice, plenty of freshly ground pepper and, if necessary, salt. Process briefly again, remembering that the final result should, like its namesake, be threadlike and not too smooth. Adjust the seasoning and turn into a bowl which, if you wish to turn out the rillettes, should be lined with a piece of foil.

Cover and refrigerate for at least 2 hours before use. To serve you could decorate the rillettes with a little more thyme, some thin slices of lemon and perhaps a few strips of smoked salmon.

# Un Piatto Italiano

I couldn't resist giving it this name: firstly, the combination of colours is that of the Italian flag, and secondly, any dish that combines mozzarella, herbs and olive oil must be Italian at heart.

If you want to be more authentic, use oregano rather than thyme when making the rillettes and to decorate the dish. Oregano is one of the herbs that dries well, so if fresh is unobtainable use the dried version.

250g/8oz SALMON RILLETTES (SEE PAGE 77)
A MOZZARELLA CHEESE
1 AVOCADO PEAR
LEMON JUICE
SALT AND PEPPER
2 tbsp OLIVE OIL
FRESH OREGANO OR THYME

Make sure the rillettes are very cold and, using a hot teaspoon, make eight rounded balls and place two on each of four plates.

Cut the mozzarella into eight slices and arrange two on each of the plates.

Quarter the avocado, peel it. Cut each quarter up lengthwise but stop about 1cm/½ inch from the end. Fan out the slices and arrange on the plates. Stop the avocado discolouring by sprinkling lemon juice over it immediately.

Grind some salt and pepper over the avocado and the mozzarella and drizzle the oil over them. Finally sprinkle the mozzarella with oregano.

# Turnip Roulade with Salmon and Crème Fraîche Filling

Turnips give the roulade an elusive flavour and one that marries well with the orange and rosemary. Choose small ones that are not fibrous and don't have too pervading a smell. The roulade mixture is thickened with breadcrumbs, rather than the more traditional roux, and as a result is very quick to make. The filling is lightly set with gelatine, which if you spread it on to the roulade, and then leave it until set, means that you can roll it easily and neatly. *Serves 6 – 8.*

*For the roulade*
250g/8oz TURNIPS
5 EGGS, SEPARATED
50g/2oz FRESH BREADCRUMBS
½ tsp ROSEMARY, FINELY CHOPPED
ZEST OF ½ ORANGE
SALT AND PEPPER

Set the oven to heat to 180°C/350°F/gas 4 and prepare a 33 × 23cm/13 × 9 inch Swiss roll tin by lining the bottom with silicone or greased greaseproof paper.

Peel and trim the turnips, cut into pieces and cook in boiling salted water for 10 minutes or until tender. Drain and purée them, either in a food processor, or by pushing through a sieve. When the purée is cool, stir in the egg yolks, breadcrumbs, rosemary and orange zest and season with salt and pepper.

Add a pinch of salt to the egg whites and whisk until they are very stiff and will hold their shape. Stir a tablespoon of egg white into the roulade mixture and then, using a metal spoon, fold in the rest. Pour the mixture into the prepared tin, smooth over the top and bake for 15 minutes, or until the top is springy to the touch. Remove from the oven and leave until cool.

*For the filling*
1 tbsp ORANGE JUICE
1½ tsp GELATINE POWDER
4 tbsp LIGHT FISH OR VEGETABLE STOCK OR WHITE WINE
150ml/¼ pint CRÈME FRAÎCHE OR SOURED CREAM
ZEST OF ½ ORANGE
½ tsp VERY FINELY CHOPPED ROSEMARY
175g/6oz COOKED SALMON, FLAKED
SALT AND PEPPER

Mix the orange juice with a tablespoon of water, sprinkle over the gelatine, place over a pan of simmering water and leave until the gelatine has dissolved.

Mix the stock or wine with the crème fraîche, the orange zest and the rosemary, then stir in the melted gelatine and finally the salmon. Season to taste. When it starts to thicken, spread it over the roulade and leave until it has set before rolling it up.

Serve on its own or with a fresh tomato coulis (page 64).

# Spinach Roulade filled with Salmon and Cream Cheese

This roulade is made without flour, the mixture being held together by the spinach. It is easiest to make it with frozen chopped spinach, but there is, of course, nothing to stop you using fresh.

A version of this roulade is much used by caterers, and little thin slices look very good on a cocktail plate. For cocktails, make smaller roulades to give slices that can be handled as finger food: use a tin of approximately 25 × 18cm/10 × 7 inches and bake it in two batches.

For a first course, either serve the roulade as it is, or accompany it with a light sauce such as tomato coulis (page 64). *Serves 8*

*For the roulade*
625g/1¼lb FROZEN CHOPPED SPINACH
25g/1oz BUTTER
4 EGGS, SEPARATED
SALT, PEPPER AND NUTMEG

Let the spinach thaw and then squeeze out as much of the water as you can.

Line a Swiss roll tin of approximately 33 × 23cm/13 × 9 inches with silicone or greased greaseproof paper and preheat the oven to 190°C/375°F/gas 5.

Purée the spinach and the butter in a blender or food processor, add the egg yolks, one by one, and season to taste with salt, pepper and some nutmeg. Add a pinch of salt to the egg whites, whisk them until stiff and relax the spinach mixture by stirring or processing a spoonful into it. Fold in the rest, spoon into the prepared tin, smooth over the top and bake for 12-14 minutes, or until the centre is firm to the touch.

Wring out a tea towel in warm water, spread it on your work surface and cover it with a sheet of greaseproof paper. Remove the cooked roulade from the oven and tip it directly on to the greaseproof paper. Leave it to cool slightly, spread on the filling and, using the paper and the cloth, roll it up. Keep it wrapped in the cloth and chill until needed.

*For the filling*

250g/8oz COOKED SALMON, FLAKED
250g/8oz CREAM CHEESE
3 tbsp SINGLE CREAM OR MILK
SALT AND PEPPER

The filling can be made in a food processor or blender but if you make it in a bowl and stir with a wooden spoon the texture will be more interesting.

Put the cream cheese, cream or milk and seasonings into a bowl, beat until soft, add the salmon and continue beating until it is amalgamated.

# Salmon Paste

Jars of salmon paste to spread in sandwiches are, with the advent of so much fresh food, far less common than they used to be. This homemade version is mild tasting and multi-purpose; it does make a good sandwich, but it can also be used as a pâté, as a filling for little choux buns or, for a first course, it can be wrapped up in slices of smoked salmon.

125g/4oz COOKED SALMON
125g/4oz COOKED WHITE FISH
75g/3oz COTTAGE CHEESE
25g/1oz BUTTER
GROUND MACE
CAYENNE
SALT AND PEPPER

Cut the fish into pieces and sieve the cottage cheese. Put the fish, the cheese and the butter into a food processor or blender and process until smooth. Season to taste with mace, cayenne and salt and pepper.

# Salmon Mousse

Salmon mousse was the great mainstay of buffet parties in the early '70s, until it was pushed to one side by the arrival of nouvelle cuisine and the fashion for mousselines and quenelles. A well made mousse should not be scorned: it may not have the sophistication of a mousseline, but it is not quite so rich and is economical in its use of ingredients. It does need making with care, and to achieve a really light mousse the cream and egg whites must be added at the critical moment when the main mixture is just about to set, so that the air bubbles do not disintegrate and are trapped into the finished mousse.

If you feel very grand, you can use a smaller soufflé dish, tie a paper collar round it and fill it about 2.5cm/1inch above the top of the dish, then remove the collar just before serving the mousse to show off the wobbly pink top. I never have much success in turning the mousse out, but if you want to do so, you will need to increase the gelatine content by about half, which will make it slightly less fluffy and more substantial.

You can make the mousse with 250g/8oz leftover salmon and a light stock, sharpened up with a tablespoonful of vinegar, or you can poach 375g/12oz salmon steaks in 600ml/1 pint court bouillon (page 38), which will yield about 250g/8oz flaked salmon and a good stock for the mousse. *Serves 6 – 8.*

250g/8oz COOKED SALMON

15g/½oz BUTTER

15g/½oz FLOUR

250ml/8 fl oz COURT BOUILLON OR LIGHT STOCK

3 tsp GELATINE

1 tsp TOMATO PURÉE

SALT AND PEPPER

150ml/¼ pint DOUBLE CREAM

2 EGG WHITES

Use the butter, flour and 175ml/6fl oz of the stock to make a velouté (page 52). Take the remaining cold stock, sprinkle over the gelatine, leave until spongy and then heat over boiling water until the gelatine has melted. In a food processor purée the salmon, adding, as you go, the velouté, the tomato purée, the melted gelatine and a generous amount of salt and pepper. Turn into a bowl, refrigerate and watch it like a hawk to catch the moment it starts to set.

In a small bowl whisk the cream, and in another the egg whites, until they are stiff. Fold the cream and then the egg whites into the setting mousse, spoon it into a 1 litre/1½ pint dish and refrigerate until needed.

# Salmon Creams

These mousses make a pleasing first course and the use of fromage frais, rather than just cream, gives them both a lower fat content and a delicious tang.

Decorate them with a small sprig of watercress or a basil leaf, and serve them warm, or at room temperature, with Watercress sauce (page 62), or Tomato coulis (page 64).

175g/6oz SALMON
125ml/4fl oz SINGLE CREAM
125ml/4fl oz FROMAGE FRAIS
1 EGG PLUS 2 YOLKS
½ tsp TOMATO PURÉE
SALT AND PEPPER

Put the salmon, cream and fromage frais in the freezer for 20 minutes before use; they need to be very cold, but not frozen. Place a tin of hot water in your oven and set it to 150°C/300°F/gas 2. Grease four ramekins.

Cut the salmon into chunks, put it into a food processor and reduce to a purée. Add the other ingredients and process, for a minute or so, or until the mixture thickens and becomes slightly gelatinous. If you want to test the seasoning, bring a small pan of water to simmering point, put in a spoonful of the mixture, cook it for 30 seconds, then remove and taste.

Divide the mixture between the prepared ramekins, place in the oven in the hot water, and cook for 20 minutes. Remove them from the oven, leave to cool for a few minutes, then run a knife round the edge and turn them out.

# Ceviche

I first had ceviche, the great South American dish in which fish is marinated and 'cooked' in citrus juice, many years ago when staying with Marika Hanbury Tenison. Marika, having travelled much in Brazil with her explorer husband Robin, was perhaps the first of the modern British cookery writers to give a recipe for it and, as nobody would have known what ceviche was, she called it simply 'marinated fish'. However, it has now regained its proper name and become well known and popular.

Ceviche can be made using lime juice or lemon juice or even orange juice and, if you like, you can spice it up with a chilli pepper or chilli powder. You can make it just with salmon or, as given below, with a mixture of fish, but all the fish should be very fresh.

250g/8oz SALMON FILLET
175g/6oz LEMON SOLE OR PLAICE FILLETS
125g/4oz COD OR HADDOCK FILLET
JUICE OF 2-3 LIMES OR LEMONS
½ SPANISH ONION, FINELY CHOPPED
1 CHILLI PEPPER, DESEEDED AND FINELY CHOPPED (OPTIONAL)
1 tbsp CORIANDER SEEDS, CRUSHED
125ml/4fl oz OLIVE OIL
SALT AND PEPPER

Remove any skin and bones from the fish and cut it all into cubes. Put the cubes into a glass or ceramic dish and pour over the lime or lemon juice. Turn with a spoon to coat all the fish. Cover and refrigerate for 3-4 hours, taking it out and turning the fish halfway.

Drain off the juice and combine some of it – you may not need it all – with all the other ingredients to make the dressing. Pour the dressing over the fish and refrigerate again for another 2 hours or so.

Serve on a bed of lettuce leaves.

# Ceviche with Avocado

Avocados, also being natives of South America, are a particularly appropriate addition to Ceviche, but they can make it rather bland, and I would recommend adding some chilli.

Just before pouring the dressing over the ceviche, add to the fish the cubed flesh of two avocados. Serve it, as above, on lettuce leaves, or piled back into the avocado shells.

# Carpaccio

This is another form of ceviche and differs from the previous recipe in that the salmon is cut into escalopes, beaten into very thin slices and, having been spread over a plate, is brushed with citrus juice. However, as it is so thin it takes only a few minutes for the juice to penetrate and 'cook' the fish and the taste of the finished dish is quite different.

The escalopes are cut from the fish in much the same way as smoked salmon is sliced, and you will need a whole fillet or side of salmon. The colder the fish, the easier it is to cut. The escalopes need to be paper thin, and unless you are a real whizz at cutting it, you will need to beat it out with a rolling pin. Any leftover fish may be used in another recipe.

250-300g/8-10oz SALMON FILLET (SEE BELOW)
1-2cm/½-¾ inch PIECE GINGER
ZEST OF 1 LIME
1 tsp SUGAR
150ml/¼ pint OLIVE OIL
1 tbsp BALSAMIC VINEGAR
SALT AND PEPPER
JUICE OF 2 LIMES

Peel and finely chop the ginger and put it, the lime zest, the sugar and 50ml/2fl oz water into a small saucepan. Bring to the boil and simmer until the liquid is reduced by half. Pour it into a bowl, add the oil and vinegar, season with salt and pepper and mix well together. Keep until needed.

Cut thin slices from the salmon fillet, put them between a double layer of greaseproof paper and bang gently with a rolling pin until they have spread and are very thin. Transfer the slices to four plates: the easiest way to do this is to remove the top layer of greaseproof paper, invert the salmon on to a plate and then peel away the second layer of paper.

When all four plates are prepared, brush the lime juice over the fish. Leave for 15 minutes, by which time the salmon will have softened and become light pink. Pour over the dressing and serve. Accompany it with brown bread and butter.

# A Striped Terrine

This terrine is made with two plain mousseline mixtures: salmon and white fish. In the last few years mousselines have appeared with multi-coloured vegetable stripes, stuffings of caviar and goodness knows what else. I have reverted to the simplest version, but there is nothing to stop you branching out and changing the herb, or adding a spice or some lightly sautéed or blanched vegetables.

A mousseline is not difficult to make but, unless you are prepared to spend hours puréeing the fish with a pestle and mortar, a food processor is essential. It is also essential to keep everything very, very cold in order to stop the mixture curdling.

If the amounts given here are too much, you could always make a small terrine, just of salmon. *Serves 8.*

250g/8oz SALMON, SKINNED AND BONED
250g/8oz LEMON SOLE OR HADDOCK FILLETS, SKINNED
300ml/½ pint DOUBLE CREAM
SALT AND PEPPER
2 EGG WHITES
A FEW SPRIGS DILL

Generously butter a 900ml/1½ pint terrine or bread tin and line it with silicone paper.

Roughly chop the salmon and put it in a bowl. Do the same with the white fish and place both bowls and your food processor bowl in the freezer. Leave for about 30 minutes or until well chilled, but not frozen. Put the cream into the freezer 10 minutes before you start making the mousselines.

Start with the white fish, but keep an eye on the salmon bowl to make sure the fish doesn't freeze. Put the fish into the cold food processor bowl, add a good pinch of salt and process for a minute or until smooth. With the machine running, add an egg white and stop when it has been incorporated into the mixture. Scrape down the bowl, add a good grinding of pepper and some chopped dill and process briefly to mix them in. If the mixture shows any sign of warming, put it back in the freezer for a few minutes, otherwise carry on and add half the cream in a steady trickle through the feed tube. Stop the moment it has all been added and the mixture is firm enough to hold its shape, as overprocessing will push out the air and make the mousseline heavy. Spoon into a bowl and refrigerate. Repeat the process with the salmon.

To test the seasoning, bring a pan of water to simmering point, put in a small spoonful of the mousseline, cook it for about 30 seconds and then taste it. Stir in more salt and pepper if necessary.

Spoon half the white mixture into the prepared terrine and spread it in an even layer. Cover with half the pink mixture, followed by the remaining white and finally the pink. Smooth over the top, cover with a piece of greaseproof paper and cook in a bain-marie at

180°C/350°F/gas 4 for 30-35 minutes or until the centre is springy when touched.

Serve the terrine either hot or at room temperature, accompanied by one or two sauces, such as Beurre blanc (page 50), Tomato coulis (page 64), Samphire sauce (page 64), or Asparagus cream, made in the same way as the filling for the Salmon en croûte (page 122), but using just 250g/8oz asparagus.

# Scrambled Egg and Salmon Terrine

In *Food for the Greedy* Nancy Shaw gives not only Lord Cobham's description of scrambled eggs and salmon (see page 147), but also a recipe for cold scrambled eggs set with aspic jelly. Cold scrambled eggs and salmon are delicious but aspic jelly, or anyway the commercial kind, is too strong in flavour, so I have developed a way of making it with fromage frais and gelatine. It makes a fresh looking and fresh tasting first course.

3 EGGS
15g/½oz BUTTER
SALT AND PEPPER
75g/3oz COLD SALMON, SKINNED AND FLAKED
1 tsp GELATINE
150ml/¼ pint FROMAGE FRAIS
2 tbsp SNIPPED CHIVES
1 tbsp CHOPPED PARSLEY
LETTUCE LEAVES FOR GARNISH

You will need four ramekins. Lightly oil them inside and put in the freezer to get really cold.

Melt the butter, break in the eggs, season them and scramble them. Put them into a bowl and fold in the salmon.

Melt the gelatine in 2 tbsp water and stir in 4 tbsp fromage frais. Season to taste, then stir about half of this mixture into the scrambled eggs.

Add the rest of the fromage frais and the herbs to the remaining gelatine mixture and adjust the seasoning.

Spoon the fromage frais and gelatine into the bottom of the ramekins and return them to the freezer for a few minutes. When set spoon the egg and salmon into them and refrigerate until needed.

Just before serving arrange some lettuce leaves on four plates. Run a knife round the inside of each ramekin and turn out on to the lettuce.

# Jellied Terrine with Turbot and Salmon

This is a cheerful terrine; everything is held together by a sparkling, slightly sweet wine jelly, and the stripes with the red pepper and cucumber dice look as if they are studded with twinkling jewels.

Serve the terrine with the light herb sauce on page 63. *Serves 6 – 8 as a first course.*

175g/6oz TURBOT FILLET, SKINNED
175g/6oz SALMON FILLET, SKINNED
½ RED PEPPER
5 cm/2 inch PIECE CUCUMBER
3 LIMES
2 tbsp SUGAR
300ml/½ pint WHITE WINE
3 tsp/1 PACKET GELATINE
SALT

Generously oil a 900ml/1½ pint terrine or bread tin and put it in the freezer. Cut the fish fillets into long thin slices then cook them, either in the microwave or by poaching them in a little wine and water.

Grill the red pepper until the skin is black and charred. Leave it to cool slightly then rub off the skin and cut the flesh into tiny dice. Peel the cucumber, quarter it lengthwise, cut out and discard the seeds and also cut into dice. Grate the zest from one lime and keep it on one side, then remove and discard the remaining skin and the pith and cut out the segments of fruit. Squeeze the juice from the other two limes.

Put the sugar and the lime zest and 125ml/4fl oz water into a small pan. Heat slowly, and when the sugar has melted, raise the heat and boil for 4 minutes. Leave until cold, then strain and mix with the wine. Put 2 tbsp water into a bowl, set it over a pan of simmering water and sprinkle on the gelatine. Leave to heat, then stir until the gelatine has dissolved. Take the pan from the heat and, in order to stop it setting too quickly, leave the bowl over the cooling water. Stir the wine mixture and the lime juice into the melted gelatine, and salt to taste.

Now build up the terrine layer by layer. Each layer needs to set before the next one is added. You can either keep plunging the terrine into the freezer, but not for too long as you don't want the fish to freeze, or you can put it into the fridge. Whatever you do, keep the bowl of jellied wine over warm water so that it does not set. You can pour each layer in from a ladle or, and I find this easier, dribble it in using a bulb baster.

Pour a thin layer of the jelly mixture into the freezing terrine and put the lime segments decoratively into it. Put to set, then add another layer of jelly and sprinkle with a third of the pepper and cucumber dice. When that has set, arrange the salmon on it, cover it with jelly and put to set. Follow that with another layer of jelly and cucumber and pepper dice, then the turbot and finally the jelly and the remaining vegetable dice.

Refrigerate until needed. Turn out and serve in slices with a spoonful of sauce on the side.

# Saumon sur le Plat

This is almost 'the storybook dish' in that it is quick and easy to execute and the final result has both sophistication and subtlety. I first saw it being made by Christian Fuentes, a young French chef of great talent, who has deserted his home in Antibes to come and work in London.

The salmon needs to be cut very thinly and from a whole fillet, as for Carpaccio (page 85). For real delicacy use an olive oil that is fruity and of the very best quality.

250-300g/8-10oz VERY THIN SALMON ESCALOPES
3 tbsp OLIVE OIL
SALT AND PEPPER
2 tbsp CHOPPED DILL

Divide the escalopes between four pieces of greaseproof paper, cover with four more pieces of paper and bang lightly with a rolling pin until the salmon is almost paper thin.

Put four plates to heat in a hot oven. Put the olive oil into small pan and place it over a gentle heat.

Five minutes before serving, remove the plates from the oven and spread them out. You must now work quickly as you do not want the plates to cool down too much. Using about two-thirds of the oil, pour a little on to each plate and use a brush to make sure the surface is covered.

Remove the top layer of greaseproof paper from each packet of salmon, turn on to the plates and peel away the other piece of greaseproof. Return the plates to the oven; a minute should be enough. Take them out again and you will see that the salmon has changed colour and cooked. Grind on salt and pepper, drizzle with the remaining oil and sprinkle with the dill. Serve immediately.

# Glazed Tartlets

These tartlets make a very decorative first course. Individual tins (7cm/4 inches across) can be bought at most kitchen shops, but you could easily use a quiche tin and make one large tart. Otherwise, little ones are attractive to serve with drinks or as part of a mixed hors d'oeuvre. They can be made in small mince pies or jam tart tins.

I like to make these with the cheese pastry I give for the Carrot, calabrese and salmon flan on page 134, but the quantity is probably a little too much for four tartlets. If you use any leftover pastry to line an extra tin or two, remember to increase the amount of filling you make. Otherwise make some shortcrust pastry or use a packet of frozen.

Small packets of aspic jelly don't seem to exist, but use half a packet and tightly seal it for future use.

*For the pastry*
Make the pastry following the directions on page 134, or following your usual recipe for shortcrust pastry. Alternatively, defrost a packet of frozen pastry.

Divide the pastry into four balls, flatten the top of each one, wrap in foil and re-frigerate for 20 minutes.

Take them from the fridge and roll each one out into a thin circle. Line the tins, and trim off the pastry edges with the rolling pin. Prick the bases with a fork, line each tin with foil and refrigerate again for 20 minutes. If you have leftover pastry, gather it up, turn it into a ball or balls and line another tin or two.

Bake the tartlet cases in a preheated oven at 200°C/400°F/gas 6 for 10-15 minutes, or until cooked and crisp. You can make these pastry cases ahead and store them for a day or two in an airtight tin.

*For the filling*
250g/8oz COOKED SALMON, FLAKED OR SLICED
5 tbsp MAYONNAISE
5 tbsp SOURED CREAM OR CRÈME FRAÎCHE
LEMON JUICE AND A LITTLE ZEST
SALT AND PEPPER
½ PACKET ASPIC JELLY
FEW STRANDS CHIVES

Mix together the mayonnaise and soured cream or crème fraîche, sharpen with a little lemon juice and season to taste.

Melt the aspic jelly in 125ml/4fl oz boiling water. Put 2 tbsp melted jelly in a bowl and cool until tepid in the fridge or freezer. Add a further 50ml/2fl oz very hot water to the re-maining jelly and leave it to cool more slowly.

Stir the tepid aspic jelly into the mayonnaise mixture and spoon it into the tartlets. Arrange the salmon on the top and sprinkle with a few snipped chives and little curls of lemon peel (use a zester).

Check the cooling jelly and just as it is about to set, dribble it over the salmon. Use no more than is needed to give a good shine, and discard the rest. Leave to set.

# Stir-fried Salmon with Asparagus

Combining Western ingredients with Eastern methods and condiments is a trend that was originally developed, largely under the influence of Chinese immigrants, on the West Coast of America. As a form of cooking it is often referred to as East meets West, and this recipe is a lovely example of why it has become so popular and of how one culture can influence and complement another.

500g/1lb ASPARAGUS
300g/10oz SALMON, SKINNED AND BONED
2 tbsp SUNFLOWER OIL
LEMON JUICE
1 tbsp SOY SAUCE
SALT AND PEPPER

Cut any tough stalks from the asparagus and then slice it, diagonally, into pieces about 1cm/½ inch long. Bring a large pan of water to the boil, salt it well and blanch the asparagus for 1½ minutes. Drain and run a cold tap over the colander to set the colour and arrest the cooking.

Cut the salmon into strips, approximately 3mm × 2.5cm/⅛ × 1 inch.

Heat the oil in a wok or large frying pan. Add the asparagus and stir-fry for about 30 seconds, then add the salmon, a squeeze of lemon juice, the soy sauce and some salt and pepper. Continue stir-frying for another 2 minutes or until the salmon is just cooked, but try not to let it disintegrate into flakes. Check the seasonings; add more if necessary but don't overdo the lemon juice or soy sauce, or they will become dominant.

Spoon on to hot plates and serve immediately.

# Sweet and Sour Salmon

Sweet and sour fish is normally fried and then coated with the sauce. Salmon doesn't lend itself to this treatment, so I poach it and then use the liquid to make the sauce.

4 × 50g/2oz SALMON FILLETS, SKINNED
2 tbsp RAISINS
2 tbsp SHERRY
½ ONION, CHOPPED
PIECE LEMON GRASS, CHOPPED
FEW STALKS CORIANDER
½ STICK CINNAMON
2 tbsp DEMERARA SUGAR
2 tsp SOY SAUCE
1 tbsp WHITE WINE VINEGAR

Soak the raisins in the sherry for about half an hour. Pour 300ml/½ pint water into a wok or sauté pan. Drain and reserve the raisins and add the sherry to the pan together with the onion, lemon grass, coriander and cinnamon. Bring to a simmer and put in the fish. Cook, turning it once, for ·5 minutes, or until just cooked. Remove the salmon to a serving dish.

Add the raisins, sugar, soy sauce and vinegar to the pan and bring to the boil. Boil fast until the sauce has reduced and become syrupy, then strain it and pour it over the salmon. Use a teaspoon to retrieve the raisins and add them to the dish.

Serve cold.

# Salmon Niçoise

Make a salad with cooked green beans and new potatoes and a few strips of grilled and skinned red pepper. Toss the salad with some of the dressing and arrange it on individual plates. Place a piece of cold, skinned and boned salmon in the centre of each plate, sprinkle on a few toasted pinenuts and the remaining dressing.

*For the dressing*
4 tbsp OLIVE OIL
1 tbsp RED WINE VINEGAR
1 CLOVE GARLIC, CRUSHED
SALT AND PEPPER

# Oriental Salad

For the salad use a mixture of watercress, sliced mooli or white radish, blanched mange-touts, chopped spring onions and, if available, sliced water chestnuts.

Arrange the salad on plates or, better still, in a decorative circle on a large platter, place some cold flaked salmon in the centre and spoon over the dressing.

*For the dressing*
½ × 150g/5oz PACKET SILKEN TOFU
1 SMALL CUCUMBER
1 CLOVE GARLIC
SALT AND PEPPER

Peel and roughly chop the cucumber and garlic. Put them into a food processor or blender, add the tofu and process until smooth. Season and refrigerate until needed.

# Pasta, Artichoke and Salmon Salad

A lovely salad. This quantity makes a first course for four, or a main course for two. In the summer and if you feel extravagant, replace the artichoke bottoms with asparagus (see below).

Use small pasta shapes such as farfalle (butterflies) or ruote (wheels).

175g/6oz PASTA SHAPES
4 CANNED ARTICHOKED BOTTOMS
175g/6oz COOKED SALMON
4 tbsp OLIVE OIL
1 tbsp SHERRY OR BALSAMIC VINEGAR
SALT AND PEPPER
1 tbsp CHOPPED PARSLEY

Use the oil and vinegar to make a dressing and season it with salt and pepper. Cut the artichoke bottoms into dice and leave them to marinate in the dressing for an hour or so.

Follow the directions on the packet to cook the pasta, then drain it and, to stop it sticking together, rinse under a cold tap.

Flake the salmon, mix it with the pasta and the artichoke bottoms and dressing. Spoon on to plates and sprinkle with parsley.

# Pasta, Asparagus and Salmon Salad

Use the same ingredients as above but replace the artichokes with 250g/8oz asparagus.

Cook the pasta as above.

Trim the asparagus, then steam or boil it until tender. Cut it into 2.5-5cm/1-2 inch lengths and keep the tips on one side.

Make a dressing with the oil and vinegar and season with salt and pepper.

Flake the salmon, mix it with the pasta, the asparagus except the tips, and about two-thirds of the dressing. Spoon the salad on to plates, arrange the reserved asparagus tips on the top, spoon on the remaining dressing and sprinkle with parsley.

# Stir-fried Salad

Stir-frying the mangetouts, sweetcorn and salmon fuses the flavours and adds interest to the salad. If you like strong flavours you could add a few drops of sesame oil to the dressing.

This is good served on a bed of cellophane noodles (transparent oriental noodles).

250g/8oz CELLOPHANE NOODLES
1cm/½ inch PIECE GINGER
2 SPRING ONIONS
125g/4oz MANGETOUTS
125g/4oz BABY SWEETCORN
250g/8oz SALMON, SKINNED AND BONED
2 tbsp SUNFLOWER OIL

*For the dressing*
2 tbsp SUNFLOWER OIL
1 tbsp SOY SAUCE

Make the dressing by whisking together the oil, soy sauce and 1 tbsp water.

Peel the ginger and chop it finely. Discard the green part of the spring onions and slice the white parts into rings. Top and tail the mangetouts and cut each baby sweetcorn diagonally into three or four. Cut the salmon into 5mm-1cm/¼-½ inch cubes.

Heat the oil in the wok, add the ginger and spring onion and stir-fry for 30 seconds. Add the mangetouts and sweetcorn, stir-fry for a further 30 seconds, then add 4 tbsp water, continue stir-frying, and when the water has nearly evaporated, add the salmon. Stir-fry for a further minute or until the fish is just cooked. Remove the wok from the heat, stir in the dressing, transfer the salad to a dish and leave to cool.

Oriental noodles often have cooking directions on the packet and if yours does, follow them. They will probably need no more than a few minutes soaking in very hot water, and the exact time varies according to the thickness of the noodles. Drain them and put them in a large bowl of cold water along with a few ice cubes and refrigerate until needed.

When you are ready to eat drain the noodles and arrange them on plates in nests. Spoon the salad into the centre.

## Fish Salad with a Thai Dressing

For this salad mix together a couple of deseeded and diced tomatoes, a few inches of peeled and diced cucumber, some beansprouts and 3-4 chopped spring onions. Add some flaked salmon and a few cooked prawns, toss together and refrigerate for half an hour. Serve garnished with a little coriander.

*For the dressing*
1 tbsp RICE VINEGAR
1 tbsp LIGHT SOY SAUCE
1½ tbsp NAM PLA OR FISH SAUCE
1 tbsp SESAME OIL
JUICE OF ½ LEMON
½ tsp CHILLI SAUCE
¼ tsp WHITE SUGAR

## Salmon with Cheese and a Walnut Dressing

Make a salad using green or red leaves, some sliced courgettes, a handful of coarsely chopped parsley and some walnut pieces.

Cut some Bel Paese, Chaumes, or similar soft cheese, and some cold salmon into cubes. Add them and the dressing to the salad and toss gently.

*For the dressing*
3 tbsp OLIVE OIL
1 tbsp WALNUT OIL
1 tbsp WHITE WINE VINEGAR
SALT AND PEPPER

# STEAKS AND PIECES OF FILLET

Salmon steaks and pieces of fillet are very adaptable and are easily transformed into supper or dinner party dishes.

These recipes are mostly very simple and several of them take no more than ten minutes to cook. The ingredients listed are for four people but the use of steaks or fillets means that the recipes can be adjusted easily for different numbers.

## *Chaudfroid of Salmon*

A chaudfroid is made by adding gelatine to mayonnaise, covering the fish with it and just before it sets, decorating the top with sprigs of herb or pieces of lemon. It is really just a glamorous way of serving salmon and mayonnaise, but one that is good for a party as the prepared salmon can be set out on a dish and easily served.

After skinning and boning don't re-assemble the steaks but decorate each half separately. Use a well seasoned mayonnaise and preferably one made with a proportion of olive oil.

For a first course or as part of a buffet this dish will be enough for eight.

4 SALMON STEAKS
1½ tsp GELATINE
300ml/½ pint MAYONNAISE

Poach, steam or microwave the salmon and leave until cold. Skin the steaks, divide each one into two, and take out the bones. Place the salmon on a wire rack and put a plate underneath it to catch any drips of mayonnaise.

Dissolve the gelatine in a couple of tablespoons of water and fold it into the mayonnaise. It will set very quickly, so spoon it immediately over the pieces of salmon. If necessary, you can smooth it over with a palette knife that has been dipped in very hot water. Decorate the top and keep cold until needed.

To serve, lift each steak on to a plate and serve as it is, with a sprig of basil for decoration or with some lettuce leaves and a small dollop of mayonnaise.

Teriyaki glazed salmon

# Cold Spiced Salmon

This sauce uses the luxury aromatic spices, saffron and cardamom. In India, presumably to remind one of its Persian origin, the sauce is referred to as Iranyi.

The teaspoonful of chilli powder makes a fairly hot sauce, so use less if you like it mild.

4 PIECES SALMON FILLET, SKINNED
½ tsp CUMIN
1 tsp RED CHILLI POWDER
SALT AND PEPPER
125ml/4fl oz CREAM
250ml/8fl oz YOGHURT
6 CARDAMOM PODS
GOOD PINCH SAFFRON STRANDS
2 tbsp OIL
1cm/½ inch PIECE GINGER, PEELED AND FINELY CHOPPED
2 CLOVES GARLIC, CRUSHED

Mix together the cumin, chilli powder and a good grinding of pepper and rub it into the salmon.

Put the cream and yoghurt into a bowl. Take the seeds from the cardamom pods and stir them in, together with the saffron and some salt.

Heat the oil in a frying pan. Add the ginger and garlic and the moment they start to sizzle put in the salmon. Cook the fish, for 15-20 seconds a side, or until it is just coloured, then add the cream and yoghurt mixture. Turn the heat down and cook the fish with the sauce just bubbling. It will take, depending on thickness, around 3-4 minutes a side.

Remove the fish to a dish. Bubble up the sauce and cook until it has reduced and thickened. Pour it over the salmon. Cover the dish, allow to cool, and refrigerate until needed.

Filo pie with salmon and Jerusalem artichokes

# Baked Salmon with Fennel and Orange

Fennel and orange go together well, and both flavours compliment salmon.

4 SALMON STEAKS
1 BULB FENNEL
150ml/¼ pint WHITE WINE
ZEST AND JUICE OF 1 ORANGE
50g/2oz BUTTER
SALT AND PEPPER

Trim the fennel of its feathery fronds and any tough outside leaves. Cut into thin slices and boil them in salted water for 4-6 minutes, or until just tender. Drain and keep.

Put the wine and the orange zest and juice into a small saucepan and simmer until the liquid has been reduced by about half. Strain, and keep on one side.

Choose an ovenproof dish that will hold the salmon steaks in one layer. Butter the dish well, lay the fennel over the bottom and sprinkle it lightly with salt and pepper. Place the salmon steaks on top, dot them with butter and sprinkle with salt and pepper. Pour on the wine and orange reduction, cover the dish tightly with foil, and bake in a preheated oven at 180°C/350°F/gas 4 for 20 minutes.

# Cold Salmon with a Pernod Sauce

The Pernod seems to mellow as the sauce cools, and even if you loathe aniseed you might appreciate this easy and surprisingly subtle way of serving cold salmon.

4 SALMON STEAKS OR SKINNED PIECES OF FILLET
50g/2oz BUTTER
2 tbsp PERNOD
2 tbsp CREAM
2 tbsp YOGHURT
1-3 tsp FINELY CHOPPED FENNEL FRONDS OR DILL, OR ½ tsp DRIED DILL WEED
SALT AND PEPPER

Melt the butter in a nonstick frying pan, then take it from the heat and swirl in 1tbsp Pernod. Put in the salmon and turn it so that it is well covered in butter and Pernod. Cover the pan and leave, off the heat, for 20-30 minutes.

Return it to the heat and cook the salmon very gently, with the pan still covered, for 4-5 minutes a side or until a fork slides easily into the flesh.

Remove the salmon, skin and, if necessary, bone it, and keep until needed. Put the pan back on the heat, deglaze with the remaining Pernod and when it has stopped sizzling stir in the cream. Cook, stirring for a minute or so, and when the sauce has amalgamated, take the pan from the hob. Leave to cool slightly, then stir in the yoghurt, the fennel or dill and season.

Arrange the salmon pieces in a shallow serving dish and pour over the sauce. Cover and refrigerate until needed.

# Salmon with Samphire

Samphire, with its bright green polyp-like stems, grows in the salt marshes along the Norfolk coast. Its season is short, mid-June to early August, but if you live or holiday in Norfolk, put on your wellingtons and go on a picking spree: a lovely expedition with the smell of the sea, the sounds of the birds, and if you are lucky, the sight of the seals.

Samphire can occasionally be found outside Norfolk and is usually sold, not by greengrocers, but by fishmongers. It may look expensive, but it weighs light, so not much is needed.

Wash the samphire in several changes of water and pick off any tough brown stems. Steam it and eat it like asparagus or as a delicious accompaniment to fish. It also makes a very appropriate and attractive decoration to a platter of cold salmon.

The simple recipe for salmon with samphire I give below can be eaten with just a few new potatoes and a pat of butter, but it is better with a Hollandaise sauce (page 44), or best of all with a saffron flavoured Hollandaise sauce (page 46), which also has the bonus of a wonderful colour combination.

4 SALMON STEAKS OR SKINNED PIECES OF FILLET
300g/10oz SAMPHIRE
PEPPER

The best way to cook salmon and samphire is to steam them. Lay the samphire in a steaming basket, put the salmon on top, grind on a little pepper – you are very unlikely to need salt – and put on to steam. As the salmon is on top of the samphire, it will probably take a little longer than suggested on page 33, and I would allow around 8-9 minutes per 2.5cm/1 inch thickness of fish. The samphire will take 12-15 minutes, and if the salmon is ready first just remove it to warm plates, leaving the samphire to finish cooking before arranging it round the salmon.

# Warm Salad of Salmon with Mango

This recipe comes from Sri Owen who writes so well about Southeast Asian food. When I rang to ask her if I could use it she told me I was the second person to do so: I am not surprised, it is easy to make and has beautifully balanced flavours. Sri Owen suggests serving it with tagliatelle tossed in a little butter.

Use a large ripe mango, but one that is still firm enough to slice. Nam pla or Thai fish sauce can be bought from Chinese and oriental grocers.

1 MANGO
½ tsp SALT
4 PIECES SALMON FILLET, SKINNED
2 tbsp OLIVE OIL
2 SHALLOTS, CHOPPED
1 CLOVE GARLIC, CRUSHED
½ tsp CHILLI POWDER
2.5cm/1 inch PIECE GINGER
2 tbsp WHITE WINE VINEGAR
2 tbsp NAM PLA
1 tsp DEMERARA SUGAR
2 tbsp CHOPPED CORIANDER LEAVES
MIXED GREEN SALAD LEAVES

Prepare the mango by holding it upright and taking a slice off each flat side, cutting down as near to the stone as you can, and then cutting the two smaller wedges off the ends. Skin each piece and cut into matchstick pieces. Put into a bowl, sprinkle with salt and leave in a cool place.

In a large frying pan heat the olive oil and over a high heat stir-fry the shallots, garlic and chilli for 1 minute.

Add the ginger, vinegar, nam pla and sugar and simmer for 2 minutes. Bring to the boil, put in the salmon and stir and simmer for 3-4 minutes. Add the coriander, stir again and remove from the heat. Leave with the salmon marinating in the sauce until you are ready to serve it.

In your serving dish make a bed of salad leaves, arrange the pieces of mango on them and put the salmon on the top. Pour on the sauce and serve.

# Chermoula

Chermoula, a marinade that is boiled up, reduced and served as a sauce, is eaten with fish of all kinds throughout the Maghreb, the North African Mediterranean countries. Every village has its own version, sometimes fiery hot, sometimes full of garlic and sometimes, as here, sharp and aromatic.

Like all Middle Eastern food, Chermoula is normally eaten when tepid or at room temperature and it is usually accompanied by wedges of lemon and a bowl of olives. I would add some freshly cooked couscous or warm pitta bread and follow it with a crisp, cool salad.

4 SALMON STEAKS OR SKINNED PIECES OF FILLET
A LITTLE FLOUR
3 tbsp OIL
2 tsp HONEY

*for the marinade*
1 SMALL ONION, THINLY SLICED
SMALL HANDFUL CORIANDER LEAVES, CHOPPED
JUICE OF 1 LEMON
1 tsp CUMIN
1 tsp PAPRIKA
1 tsp GROUND CINNAMON
¼ tsp CAYENNE
1 tsp SALT

Put the salmon into a shallow dish.

Mix together all the marinade ingredients and add 2 tbsp water. Pour the marinade over the salmon and leave, turning the fish once or twice, for around 4 hours.

Remove the salmon, scraping the marinade back into the dish. Use a piece of kitchen paper to pat the fish dry, then dredge it with a little flour. In a frying pan heat the oil, put in the salmon and gently fry for around 3 minutes each side, or until light golden and barely cooked. Remove the salmon to a plate. Discard all but 1 tbsp oil from the pan, then add the marinade, the honey and 3 tbsp water. Bring it to the boil and simmer for around 5 minutes or until the onion is soft and the sauce is starting to become syrupy.

Put the salmon back into the pan and cook for 1 minute on each side. Remove to a dish, spoon the sauce over it and leave to cool.

# Poached Salmon with Pineau des Charentes

Pineau des Charentes is the latest French aperitif to appear on the British market. It comes, as you might guess, from the Charentes, and is made from grape juice blended with brandy. It is sweet and fruity, but cut with a curiously bitter twinge, and when chilled, it makes a very satisfying drink. It is equally satisfying to use in the kitchen and adds an unusual taste to a simple sauce.

4 SALMON STEAKS OR SKINNED PIECES OF FILLET
300ml/½ pint FISH OR VEGETABLE STOCK
75ml/3fl oz PINEAU DES CHARENTES
75ml/3fl oz CRÈME FRAÎCHE OR SOURED CREAM
SALT AND PEPPER

Pour the stock and Pineau des Charentes into a wide pan and bring it to a simmer. Add the salmon and cook, turning once, for 8-10 minutes or until just done. Remove the fish to a plate, cover and keep in a low oven.

Bring the liquid in the pan to the boil and let it bubble for around 5 minutes or until it has reduced by at least half and is starting to turn syrupy. Stir in the crème fraîche or soured cream, bring back to the boil and bubble for another minute or two. Season, if necessary, with salt and pepper.

Pour a pool of sauce into the centre of four warm plates and place a piece of salmon in the middle.

# Grilled Salmon with a Mustard Paste

A mild mustard goes well with salmon (think of gravad lax sauce), and is the basis for this paste, which is spread over the fish just before it is grilled. I wanted to jazz it up a little, so I poured in some soy sauce: it worked.

4 SALMON STEAKS OR SKINNED PIECES OF FILLET
1-2 SPRING ONIONS
2 tbsp DIJON MUSTARD
1 tbsp LEMON JUICE
1 tbsp SOFT BROWN SUGAR
1 tbsp SOY SAUCE

Using the white parts only finely chop the spring onion or onions. Put the onion into a bowl and stir in the mustard, lemon juice, sugar and soy sauce.

Heat your grill. Put the salmon steaks or fillets on the grill rack and annoint them with about half of the mustard mixture. Grill for 4 minutes, turn the fish and spread on the remaining mustard. Return to the grill and leave until cooked.

# Poached Salmon Fillet with a Saffron Sauce

In the best tradition of nouvelle cuisine, the sauce for this dish is reduced, then thickened with cream and finally butter. It is rich, but I have cut down by using single cream and just a knob of butter; the sauce still tastes very good.

I like to serve this with tagliatelle and spinach; they both go well with the saffron sauce.

4 PIECES SALMON FILLET, SKINNED
GOOD PINCH SAFFRON THREADS
150ml/¼ pint LIGHT FISH OR VEGETABLE STOCK
50ml/2fl oz WHITE WINE
200ml/7fl oz SINGLE CREAM
15-25g/½-1oz BUTTER
SALT AND PEPPER

*To serve*
250g/8oz TAGLIATELLE
1kg/2lb FRESH SPINACH OR 500g/1lb FROZEN

If serving spinach and tagliatelle cook the spinach and keep it warm, and put the water to boil for the tagliatelle.

Put the saffron to soak in a small bowl in 2 tbsp warm water.

In a sauté or frying pan bring the stock and the wine to simmering point and gently poach the fish for 3-4 minutes a side. When it is just cooked, remove it to a dish, cover and keep warm.

Put the tagliatelle to cook and continue with making the sauce.

Add the saffron to the pan, then raise the heat and bubble until the liquid has reduced by about half. Stir in the cream, bring back to simmering point, and reduce it by a further third or until it starts to thicken. Whisk in the butter, season with salt and pepper.

Drain the tagliatelle and arrange it in nests on the plates. Spoon the spinach into the centre, top it with a piece of salmon and drizzle the sauce over the top.

# Grilled Salmon with Breadcrumb Crust

This recipe, which is easy, quick and very good, comes from Marie-Pierre Moine, the author of that lovely book *Cuisine Grand-mère*. I jotted it down while on the telephone, on a scrap of paper with a blunt pencil, so I hope she will forgive me if this varies from her original: the shallot, I know, is my addition.

500g/1lb PIECE SALMON FILLET, SKINNED
1 SHALLOT, FINELY CHOPPED
LARGE HANDFUL PARSLEY, FINELY CHOPPED
75g/3oz FINE BREADCRUMBS
SALT AND PEPPER
OLIVE OIL
JUICE OF 1 LEMON

Mix together the shallot, parsley and breadcrumbs, and season with salt and pepper.

Heat your grill. Place the salmon, skinned side upwards, on the grill tray, brush it with olive oil, squeeze on some lemon juice and cook, keeping it a few inches from the flame to stop it browning too much, for 4 minutes. Turn the salmon over, brush the un-cooked side with olive oil and lemon juice, then cover with the breadcrumbs. Drizzle a little more oil over the top and return it to the grill for a further 3-4 minutes, or until the top is brown and a knife slides easily through the fish.

# Teriyaki Glazed Salmon

Teriyaki sauce is much used in Japan as a glaze for grilled or pan-fried beef, chicken or fish. It is a sweet sauce based on soy sauce. Look for one made with Japanese rather than Chinese soy sauce.

This is best served with stir-fried vegetables; they add bite and mix well with the sweet sauce.

4 PIECES SALMON FILLET, WITH THE SKIN ON
2 tbsp SOY SAUCE
1 tbsp RICE WINE OR SWEET SHERRY
1 tbsp SUGAR
1 tsp FINELY CHOPPED GINGER

In a small pan combine the soy sauce, rice wine or sherry, the sugar and the ginger. Heat it slowly and then cook gently for 2 or 3 minutes or until it becomes slightly syrupy. Don't let it boil away. Allow to cool and keep until required.

Heat your grill and place the fillets on a rack skin side down. Grill them for 1 minute then turn and grill for 3 minutes or until the skin is crisp and the fish nearly cooked. Turn again, brush the top with the Teriyaki sauce, and return to the grill for a further minute. Put the salmon on heated plates and drizzle any remaining sauce over it.

# Salmon in Coconut Milk Sauce

An aromatic coconut milk sauce appears frequently as an accompaniment to fish in Southeast Asian cuisine, and it transfers well to salmon or other Western fish. This recipe is based on one using monkfish in Jill Norman's *The Complete Book of Spices*. She specifies using chilli powder, but I find it slightly too strong against the combination of salmon and the other spices, so I leave it out. Creamed coconut can be bought in packets at many delicatessens or specialist shops.

4 FILLETS SALMON, SKINNED
75g/3oz CREAMED COCONUT
1 SHALLOT, FINELY CHOPPED
1 CLOVE GARLIC, FINELY CHOPPED
3cm/½ inch FRESH GINGER, FINELY CHOPPED
3 CARDAMOM PODS
½ tsp GROUND CUMIN
SALT AND PEPPER
1 STALK LEMON GRASS

Crumble the creamed coconut into 150ml/¼ pint very hot water and stir to dissolve. Stir in the shallot, garlic and ginger.

Remove the seeds from the cardamom pods and crush them to a powder. Mix them with the cumin, and a good grinding of black pepper. Rub it into the salmon fillets and leave on one side. Cut off and discard the outer leaves from the lemon grass and thoroughly crush the inner stalk.

Pour the coconut milk into a sauté pan, add the lemon grass, bring to the boil and simmer gently until the sauce has thickened and reduced by about half. Remove the lemon grass, season the sauce with salt and then add the salmon fillets, turning to coat with sauce. Cook them, turning once more, for 6-8 minutes or until they are just done, then remove to hot plates, spoon the remaining sauce over the top and serve immediately.

# Pan-fried Salmon with a Tarragon Sauce

Pan-frying salmon, offers enormous scope; the fish can easily be cooked individually or in larger quantities, and kept warm while making a sauce in the pan. For this reason pan-fried salmon is often on restaurant menus. I give three recipes and variations.

The sauce given here uses the happy combination of dry vermouth, tarragon and tomato, but other herbs and flavourings can be just as effective and I follow the recipe with some suggestions.

4 SALMON STEAKS OR SKINNED PIECES OF FILLET
SALT AND PEPPER
25g/1oz BUTTER
1 SHALLOT OR ½ SMALL ONION, FINELY CHOPPED
2 tbsp DRY VERMOUTH
300ml/½ pint FISH OR LIGHT VEGETABLE STOCK
SMALL HANDFUL TARRAGON LEAVES
2 tbsp DOUBLE CREAM
1 TOMATO, PEELED, DESEEDED AND CUT INTO STRIPS

Lightly season the salmon with salt and pepper. Heat half the butter in a nonstick pan and, when it is hot, seal the salmon by cooking it for about a minute on each side. Turn the heat down, and if the fish is thick, cover the pan. Cook for a further 2-6 minutes, turning once. Check, by sliding in a fork, that the salmon is just cooked. Remove it to a dish, cover with foil and keep warm in a low oven.

Add the shallot or onion to the pan and cook for a couple of minutes or until soft. Sprinkle on the vermouth and when it has nearly evaporated, pour in the stock and add the tarragon. Simmer, until the liquid has reduced by half, then add the cream and tomato, and season with salt and pepper. Bring back to just below boiling point, remove the pan from the heat and swirl in the remaining butter to thicken the sauce and give it an attractive gloss.

Spoon the sauce on to four warm plates and place a piece of salmon in the centre.

# Pan-fried Salmon with Basil

Cook the salmon and make the sauce as given above, but use an extra tomato and white wine instead of the dry vermouth. Replace the tarragon with shredded basil leaves, but do not add them to the sauce until just before serving it.

# Pan-fried Salmon with Sorrel

Cook the salmon and make the sauce as above, leaving out the tomato and using white wine instead of the dry vermouth. Replace the tarragon with a large handful of sorrel leaves: shred them and, at the last minute, stir them into the sauce.

# Pan-fried Salmon with Lemon and Thyme

Cook the salmon and make the sauce as above, leaving out the tomato and replacing the dry vermouth with a sweet Cinzano, and the tarragon with finely chopped thyme; lemon thyme if possible.

You will also need a lemon. Add the zest to the pan at the same time as the stock and, at the end, a squeeze of juice to taste.

# Pan-fried Salmon with Cucumber Ribbons

Crisp cucumber ribbons are swirled on to a plate and topped with a piece of salmon. This is also good served as a first course, but reduce the quantities if you do so.

4 SALMON STEAKS OR SKINNED PIECES OF FILLET
2 CUCUMBERS
SALT AND PEPPER
50g/2oz BUTTER
150ml/¼ pint CRÈME FRAÎCHE OR SOURED CREAM
1 tbsp FINELY CHOPPED MINT, DILL OR BASIL

Cut the cucumbers in half and use a swivel headed potato peeler to peel them. Taking half at a time, and still using the peeler, strip off tagliatelle-like ribbons. You will find this is easiest if you turn the cucumber in your hand as you go along. When you get to the seeds discard the core.

Put the cucumber ribbons into a sieve, sprinkle with 1 tbsp salt and shake the sieve to spread it well. Leave to sweat and drain for at least half an hour.

When you are nearly ready to cook, remove the moisture from the cucumber strips by turning them on to a double layer of kitchen paper and patting dry.

Sprinkle the salmon with a very little salt and some pepper. Heat half the butter in a nonstick pan and when it is hot, quickly seal the salmon by cooking it for a minute on each side. Reduce the heat and cook, turning the fish once more, for 3-5 minutes, depending on its thickness. The moment it is cooked, take it from the pan, put it in a dish, cover and keep warm in a low oven.

Add the remaining butter to the pan and when it starts to sizzle, put in the cucumber. Cook, stirring, for 3 minutes or until the ribbons start to soften. Remove the pan from the heat, and leave it to cool slightly before stirring in the crème fraîche or soured cream, herbs and seasoning to taste.

Arrange the cucumber on four hot plates and place a piece of salmon in the middle.

# Pan-fried Salmon with Orange, Rosemary and Redcurrant Jelly

This sauce is best made with Seville oranges, but you can, when they are out of season, use the zest and juice of a sweet orange well sharpened with lemon juice.

4 SALMON STEAKS OR SKINNED PIECES OF FILLET
15g/½oz BUTTER
2 SEVILLE ORANGES, OR 1 SWEET ORANGE AND 1 LEMON
300ml/½ pint LIGHT FISH OR VEGETABLE STOCK
2 SPRIGS ROSEMARY
3 tbsp DOUBLE CREAM
1 tsp REDCURRANT JELLY
SALT AND PEPPER
½ tsp VERY FINELY CHOPPED ROSEMARY LEAVES

Heat the butter in a nonstick frying pan. Lightly season the salmon, put it into the pan and cook, to seal, for a minute a side. Turn the heat down and if the fish is thick cover the pan, and cook, turning the fish once more, until just done and a fork will slide easily into the flesh.

Remove the salmon to a plate, cover and keep warm in a low oven. Add to the pan the zest and juice of the Seville oranges or the orange and the lemon juice, the stock and rosemary sprigs. Bring to the boil, bubble until the liquid is reduced by half, then take from the heat and remove the rosemary from the pan. Add the cream and jelly and stir until the jelly melts, returning the pan briefly to the heat if necessary. Season to taste with salt and pepper adding, if the balance of the sauce needs it, more bitter orange or lemon juice or redcurrant jelly.

Spoon the sauce on to four warm plates, place a piece of salmon in the centre and sprinkle on a little chopped rosemary.

# Salmon Parcels with Wine and Mushrooms

Individual parcels are good for entertaining as they can be prepared ahead and cooked at the last minute, either in a conventional or a microwave oven. When cooking conventionally, wrap the parcels with silicone paper or foil, and when using the microwave with silicone paper. I would not recommend using greaseproof paper as it is inclined to become soggy and to look uninspiring when presented on a plate.

You can pack your parcels as given below, or you could vary the dish by using another herb, or replacing the mushrooms with a quick cooking vegetable such as courgettes.

With this recipe you can relieve the last-minute pressure by working ahead, and reducing the cream for the sauce. Keep it warm in a bain-marie, and when you place the parcels in the oven, increase the heat to boil the water and make the cream really hot.

4 SALMON STEAKS
50g/2oz BUTTER
1 SHALLOT, CHOPPED
250g/4oz BUTTON MUSHROOMS, SLICED
SALT AND PEPPER
4 tbsp WHITE WINE
150ml/¼ pint CREAM
3 tbsp CHOPPED PARSLEY

Cut out four pieces of paper or foil large enough to fold over and encase the salmon. You can use any convenient shape, but hearts are traditional as they fold into neat half moons.

Generously butter the inside of the paper or foil envelopes. Sprinkle a little of the shallot over one half of each piece of paper, heap on the mushrooms and season with salt and pepper. Cover with a salmon fillet, season it, smear it with butter, sprinkle on any remaining shallot, and moisten each one with 1 tbsp wine. Fold over the second half and seal the parcels well by turning all the edges over a couple of times. You can do this ahead, but if you cook them from the refrigerator increase the time by 2-3 minutes for an oven or 30 seconds for the microwave.

Place a baking tray in the oven, heat it to 190°C/375°F/gas 5, and cook the parcels for 15 minutes. Alternatively, put the parcels in a microwave and cook for 6 minutes. In both cases, after taking the parcels from the oven, leave them to rest for a couple of minutes before opening. While they are in the oven, boil up the cream, reduce it by about half, add the parsley, and salt and pepper to taste.

Place the cooked parcels on individual plates and slash a cross in the top of each with a knife. Fold it open and pour in some hot cream. Serve immediately with potatoes or rice to mop up the juices.

# Monkfish and Salmon Parcels with Red Pepper Butter

I call this a butter, but I haven't included it along with the others at the beginning of the book as the addition of the soft pepper means that the butter will not harden up again. The red pepper blends beautifully with both the monkfish and the salmon, but if you want to ring the changes use any of the flavoured butters on pages 40-43.

250g/8oz SALMON, SKINNED AND BONED
250g/8oz MONKFISH, SKINNED AND BONED
1 RED PEPPER
50g/2oz BUTTER
SQUEEZE OF LEMON JUICE
SALT AND PEPPER

Grill the pepper until it is black and charred all over. Put it in a plastic bag to prevent moisture loss, seal it and leave until it is cool. Skin the pepper and discard the core and seeds. Roughly chop the flesh and either mash it up with the butter or process them together in a food processor. Season to taste with a squeeze of lemon juice, salt and pepper.

Cut the salmon and the monkfish into bite size pieces.

Follow the instructions in the previous recipe to cut out pieces of foil or paper. Use some of the butter to grease the inside of the envelopes, divide the fish evenly between them and spoon the red pepper butter on top. Seal tightly and keep until needed.

Preheat the oven to 190°C/375°F/gas 5. Put the parcels on a baking tray and cook for 7 minutes. Alternatively, cook for 5 minutes in a microwave.

# Pastry Parcels of Salmon with Currants and Ginger

HOW TO BAKE A JOLL OF FRESH SALMON
Take Ginger and salt and season it, and certain Currans, and cast them about and under it and let the paste be fine, and take a little butter and lay it about the paste, and set it in the oven two houres, and serve it.
*The Good Huswife's Jewell*, Thomas Dawson, 1696

Salmon combined with currants and preserved ginger is one of the oldest dishes in English Cookery. It must have been much used, for not only did it appear as above, but a similar recipe was given in *Cooks and Confectioners' Dictionary* by John Nott, published in 1726.

It was revived, maybe not for the first time, by George Perry-Smith at his restaurant The Hole in the Wall in Bath, and Joyce Molyneux, who cooked there, still puts it on her menu at The Carved Angel in Dartmouth. After all these credits I would just add, try it, and you will see that it is no accident that it has lasted for so long.

The herb sauce is easy to make and has a light flavour that will not mask or swamp the prickle of the ginger.

*For the parcels*
SHORTRCRUST PASTRY MADE WITH 250g/8oz FLOUR
4 PIECES SALMON FILLET, SKINNED
2 KNOBS OF GINGER IN SYRUP, WELL DRAINED AND FINELY CHOPPED
1 tbsp CURRANTS
50g/2oz BUTTER, SOFTENED
SALT AND PEPPER
1 EGG YOLK, BEATEN WITH A LITTLE SALT FOR THE GLAZE

Mix the ginger and currants into the butter. Roll the pastry into a 40cm/16 inch square and cut into four 20cm/8 inch squares. Place a piece of salmon fillet in the centre of each square, sprinkle with salt and pepper and spread a quarter of the prepared butter on it. Lift two opposite corners and seal them with a little egg wash over the top of the filling. Lift the other two corners and seal them in the centre in the same way. Brush the seams with egg glaze and press together.

Put the parcels on a greased baking tray, cut a vent in the top, brush over with egg wash and bake for 25-30 minutes at 190°C/375°F/gas 5.

*For the sauce*
125g/4oz BUTTER
150ml/¼ pint DOUBLE CREAM
1 tbsp EACH CHOPPED TARRAGON, PARSLEY AND, IF AVAILABLE, CHERVIL
LEMON JUICE
SALT AND PEPPER

Melt the butter, then pour in the cream and bring to the boil. Cook for 1 minute then take from the heat and stir in the herbs. Sharpen with a squeeze of lemon juice and season to taste.

# Parsi Parcels

At Parsi weddings these parcels are traditionally made with the white fish, pomfret, wrapped in banana leaves and steamed. Salmon makes a good substitute for pomfret and foil for the banana leaves.

I have seen a recipe that uses five chillies, but I am not too keen on having the roof of my mouth blown off, so I tried it using two small ones and it was still pretty hot.

4 SALMON STEAKS
1-2 GREEN CHILLIES, DESEEDED AND CHOPPED
2 CLOVES GARLIC, CHOPPED
1 tsp GROUND CUMIN
LARGE HANDFUL FRESH CORIANDER, LEAVES ONLY
1 tbsp SUGAR
1 tsp SALT
75g/3oz CREAMED COCONUT, ROUGHLY CHOPPED
3 tbsp LEMON JUICE

Put the chillies, garlic, cumin, coriander, sugar and salt into a food processor and process until everything is very finely chopped. Add the creamed coconut and process until that too is finely chopped. Add the lemon juice and 1 tbsp boiling water and process again until you have a smooth paste.

Cut out four squares of foil, spread a little of the paste on to each and put a salmon steak on top of it. Spread the remaining paste on the steaks, and wrap up the foil.

Set the parcels in a steamer or on a rack over boiling water in a wok. Cover and steam for 20-25 minutes, depending on the thickness of the fish.

Serve with rice.

Parcels of salmon, potato and olive oil

# Oven-cooked Salmon with Red Wine and Mushrooms

'They say fish should swim thrice – first it should swim in the Sea – then it should
swim in Butter; then at last, Sirrah, it should swim in good Claret.'
(*Polite Conversation*, Jonathan Swift)

There is a Burgundian red wine sauce, sauce meurette, that is served with fish or
poached eggs and made like a coq au vin, with mushrooms, bacon and baby onions. I
find this a little strong for salmon and prefer this version with just the mushrooms. I am
also happy to follow Jonathan Swift and use a claret or any reasonable sturdy red wine.

4 SALMON STEAKS
25g/1oz FLOUR
50g/2oz BUTTER
250g/8oz BUTTON MUSHROOMS, SLICED
300ml/½ pint RED WINE
1 SHALLOT, FINELY CHOPPED
SALT AND PEPPER
1 tbsp CHOPPED PARSLEY

Preheat the oven to 180°C/350°F/gas 4 and generously grease an ovenproof dish. Make a
beurre manié by kneading together the flour and half the butter.

Put the mushrooms in the dish, lay the salmon on top of them and pour over the wine.
Sprinkle on the shallot and some salt and pepper and place a knob of butter on each
piece of salmon.

Cover the dish tightly and put it into the oven for 20 minutes, or until the salmon is
just cooked. Remove the salmon to a serving dish, keep it warm and strain the juice into
a saucepan. Heat the pan, bubble up the wine and cook for a few minutes to reduce it by
about half. Lower the heat, strain in any further juices from the mushrooms, and add the
beurre manié bit by bit, stirring all the time. When it has all been incorporated, and the
sauce has thickened, put in the mushrooms and the parsley and check the seasoning.
Pour the hot sauce over the salmon and serve.

Oeufs pochés bénédictine

# Piquant Salmon

Derek Cooper, when making his tv series 'Scotland's Larder', finished the programme on Shetland by showing Margaret Fraser cooking this dish for him.

Mrs Fraser, who lives overlooking the sea and a salmon farm, kindly sent me the complete recipe, and I give it with very little alteration. She is obviously a marvellous cook and this is a lovely example of how good salmon is when complemented with flavours and ingredients from other parts of the world.

The marinade, Margaret Fraser says, is enough for up to 1kg/2lb salmon fillet, but I made it, for four people, using 500g/1lb salmon and marinating it in half the mixture. I warmed the remaining marinade and served it as a sauce; there was none left over. Mrs Fraser warned me against overcooking the fish, saying that once it has been in a marinade it cooks extra fast and needs watching carefully.

4 PIECES SALMON FILLET, SKINNED
2-3 tbsp FLOUR
1 tbsp OIL OR CLARIFIED BUTTER

*For the marinade*
6 tbsp DRY WHITE WINE
1 tbsp WHITE WINE VINEGAR
1 tbsp GIN
½ PAPAYA
JUICE OF 1 LIME
1 tsp DIJON MUSTARD
3 tbsp YOGHURT
1 tsp SOFT BROWN SUGAR
½ tsp SALT AND A GOOD GRINDING OF PEPPER

*For the garnish*
½ PAPAYA, SLICED
1 LIME, CUT INTO WEDGES

Put all the marinade ingredients into a food processor or blender and process until smooth.

Lay the pieces of salmon fillet in a shallow dish, cover with half the marinade and leave for at least 8 hours. Turn the fish several times.

Wipe the fish dry with kitchen paper. Dust each piece with flour, and brush with a little oil or melted clarified butter. Grill for 2-3 minutes on each side.

Gently warm the unused marinade, but don't let it heat too much or it will separate.

Serve the salmon hot, garnished with the remaining half papaya and wedges of lime and with the sauce on the side.

# Salmon Cooked in Black Bean Sauce

The small black soya beans used in this recipe can be bought, salted, in tins or packets, at Chinese or Eastern shops. They are easy to cook and give this sauce an unusual and distinctive taste.

4 PIECES SALMON
1½ tbsp BLACK BEANS
2-4 SPRING ONIONS
1 tbsp OIL
1cm/½ inch PIECE GINGER, FINELY CHOPPED
1 CLOVE GARLIC, FINELY CHOPPED
2 tbsp SWEET SHERRY, OR DRY SHERRY AND 1 tsp SUGAR

*To serve*
250-300g/8-10oz beansprouts

Wash the black beans, leave them to soak for an hour or so, then drain and coarsely chop them. Trim the spring onions and cut off and chop the white part. (Keep the green ends for a salad or some other use.)

Cook the beansprouts for 3 minutes in a pan of salted water. Drain and keep warm until needed.

In a wok or wide frying pan heat the oil. Add the ginger, garlic and spring onions, stir-fry for a few seconds, then add the black beans. Continue stir-frying for a few more seconds, then mix in the sherry and, if you are using it, the sugar. Pour in 150ml/¼ pint water. Bring to simmering point, then add the salmon. Cook, turning once, for 5-6 minutes or until just cooked.

Have ready four hot plates and divide the beansprouts between them. Place a piece of salmon on top of them. Then raise the heat and, squashing down the black beans, quickly reduce the sauce. Spoon it over the salmon and serve.

# Paupiettes of Lemon Sole and Salmon

The lemon sole fillets are spread with flavoured breadcrumbs and then rolled round a piece of salmon. The paupiettes are easy to make and have the advantage that they can be prepared and then kept refrigerated for a few hours before cooking.

4 LEMON SOLE FILLETS, SKINNED
4 SMALL PIECES SALMON FILLET, SKINNED
2 tbsp MILK
25g/1oz FRESH BREADCRUMBS
2 tbsp PINENUTS
2 tbsp BASIL, FINELY SHREDDED
SALT AND PEPPER

Pour the milk over the breadcrumbs and leave to soak. Lightly toast the pinenuts, either under a grill or by tossing them over a medium heat in a small frying pan. Roughly chop the pinenuts with a knife or pulse them briefly three or four times in a food processor. Stir the pinenuts and basil into the breadcrumbs and season well.

Lay out the lemon sole fillets skinned side upwards, sprinkle them lightly with salt and pepper and spread on the breadcrumb mixture. Put a piece of salmon on top of each and roll them up.

Take four pieces of foil and brush each one with oil. Wrap up the paupiettes into a sausage shape, making certain that the foil is well sealed. Bring a pan of water to the boil, put in the foil sausages and simmer for 8 minutes. Remove from the pan, unwrap the paupiettes and place on hot plates.

Serve with the Warm tomato dressing, page 65.

# WHOLE SALMON
# AND PARTY DISHES

In this chapter I give recipes for large cuts or for whole fish cooked along with accompanying flavours: stuffed, cooked in pastry or, in one recipe, steamed and served with stir-fried vegetables. The recipes are fairly time-consuming and one or two of them quite complicated, but they are all satisfying both to make and serve.

Plainly cooked whole salmon for parties is dealt with at the beginning of the book (see pages 26-35); sauces for a plain salmon can be found on pages 39-65.

## *Coulibiac*

Kulebyaka, or coulibiac as we now usually call it, was originally made with sturgeon, and the filling was bound together with *vesiga*, a gelatinous compound made from the spinal cord of the fish. But times change, and nowadays a coulibiac is nearly always made with salmon, and pastry, not vesiga, is relied upon to hold the whole thing together.

The filling always seems to include mushrooms and hardboiled eggs, and these and the salmon are layered with rice or a grain product. In Russia, rice would have been expensive, and probably used only by the grand chefs in St Petersburg. When the aristocrats returned to their country estates for the long summer break, it would have been replaced with a home-grown grain such as buckwheat, millet or semolina.

In this recipe I have used semolina, both because I like its texture and because I find it blends sympathetically with the other filling ingredients. I also like the extravagance of stirring some chopped smoked salmon into it, as suggested by Margaret Costa in her *Four Seasons Cookbook*. Coulibiac is best made with fillets of fresh salmon, which are then very lightly cooked, but a passable one can also be made using cold cooked salmon.

The authentic and the best coulibiac is made with a brioche dough, and after lots of frustration and wasted eggs, I have found a way of making this with fast-acting yeast in a food processor. The amount of yeast may sound a lot but it is needed to counteract the butter and eggs in the dough. The dough is very quick to make and the result is so much better than resorting to a packet of frozen. *Serves 8-10.*

*For the brioche dough*
275g/9oz STRONG WHITE FLOUR
1 × 7g/¼oz PACKET FAST ACTION DRIED YEAST
½ tsp SALT
½ tsp SUGAR
2 EGGS
3 tbsp WARM MILK
125g/4oz VERY SOFT BUTTER

Put the flour, yeast, salt and sugar into the bowl of your food processor. With the motor running add the eggs and then the milk through the feed tube. Continue processing until the dough forms a ball round the central knife, then leave the machine on to knead it for a further 15-20 seconds.

Remove the dough and knead by hand for 2-3 minutes, or until it is elastic and smooth. Tear it up into pieces, and put them into the food processor along with the butter. Process again and stop the machine when the dough has reformed. It will be very sticky. Remove and knead by hand for a further 2-3 minutes or until smooth. Put it into an oiled bowl, cover with clingfilm, put in the fridge and leave to rise for several hours or overnight.

*For the filling*
300ml/½ pint MILK
50g/2oz SEMOLINA
SALT AND PEPPER
50-75g/2-3oz SMOKED SALMON, CHOPPED (OPTIONAL)
900g/2lb TAILPIECE SALMON, OR 625g/1¼lb BONED AND SKINNED SALMON
FILLET, OR 625g/1¼lb COLD SALMON
125g/4oz BUTTER
1 SHALLOT OR ½ SMALL ONION, CHOPPED
125g/4oz MUSHROOMS, SLICED
3 HARDBOILED EGGS, SLICED
3 tbsp CHOPPED PARSLEY

*To finish*
1 EGG BEATEN WITH A PINCH OF SALT
2 tbsp DRY BREADCRUMBS
50g/2oz BUTTER

*To serve*
300ml/½ pint SOURED CREAM
1 tbsp CHOPPED PARSLEY
SMALL BUNCH CHIVES
SALT, PEPPER AND PAPRIKA

Bring the milk to boiling point, sprinkle in the semolina and some salt and pepper and stir, over a low heat, until the mixture thickens. Remove from the heat and stir in the smoked salmon, if using. Cover the semolina and leave until needed.

If you are using a salmon tail, skin and bone it. Using a sharp knife, cut the tailpieces or fillets lengthwise into thick slices. Heat half the butter in a nonstick frying pan and fry the salmon for minute or two each side, or until it has stiffened and is lightly cooked. If you are using cold salmon, skin it and divide it into pieces.

Melt the remaining butter in the frying pan, add the shallot or onion and cook gently until transparent, then stir in the mushrooms and cook until any moisture that comes from them has evaporated. Take the pan from the heat, leave until the contents have cooled, and then mix in the eggs and parsley and season to taste.

Take the dough from the fridge, punch it down, then roll it out into a rectangle approximately 25 × 40cm/10 × 16 inches. To make it easier to obtain a neat sausage cut a 5cm/2 inch square from each corner. Leaving a wide border so that the pastry can be folded over and wrapped round the filling, spread the semolina down the centre of the dough. Cover it neatly with the salmon pieces and top it with the egg and mushroom mixture. Dampen the edges of the dough with a little water, fold up the long sides so that they just overlap, and press them together. Complete the parcel by turning up the ends. Make sure that all the joins are well sealed.

Transfer the coulibiac to a greased baking sheet, either by lifting it or by rolling it on to something like a piece of foil and lifting it that way. Make sure that the joins are underneath.

Cover and leave it in a warm place for around half an hour. Heat the oven to 200°C/400°F/gas 6. Make three or four angled cuts across the top of the coulibiac and cut two or three holes between them. Brush with the egg glaze and sprinkle with the dry breadcrumbs.

Bake for 35-40 minutes, or until well risen and golden brown. Remove from the oven and pour melted butter in through the holes. Leave to cool for 10 minutes or so, then cut into slices.

Mix the soured cream with the parsley and snipped chives and season with salt, pepper and paprika. Hand the cream separately when serving the coulibiac.

# Salmon en Croûte

A party dish that is both rich and glamorous. Make it in a fish shape, which is not nearly as difficult as you might think, and decorate it with scales, a tail, a beady eye and a beautiful smile.

I have a summer birthday, which I share with a great friend, and one year we decided on a celebration *déjeuner sur l'herbe*. It fell to me to make the salmon en croûte, but after consulting endless recipes, I decided to branch out and follow none of them. This dish of salmon fillets sandwiched together with a tarragon flavoured mousseline, wrapped in pastry and served with a beurre blanc, was the result. Extraordinarily, it made marvellous, slightly grand, plate and fork picnic food.

I have an absolute hatred of cold puff pastry and was determined not to subject the picnickers to that, so I assembled it ahead, kept it in a cold fridge and cooked it at the last minute, making the beurre blanc while it was in the oven. I then wrapped it in several layers of foil and a blanket and poured the beurre blanc into a wide mouthed thermos. Two hours later it emerged, still warm and crisp and with the perfect sauce to go with it.

You will need a template in the shape of a fat, wide tailed fish. The easiest way to achieve an even fish is to fold a large piece of paper down the middle, and keeping the crease as the centre line of the fish, to draw one side of it. Leave it folded, cut it out and then open it up. For this recipe you will need a template around 32-35cm/13-14 inches long and 18-20cm/7½-8 inches wide.

The salmon needs to be filleted, very carefully boned and then skinned. You can use frozen puff pastry: you will need two 250g/8oz pieces and, to get it big enough, you will have to roll the top or covering piece until it is very thin. Otherwise, and it is worth it for such a special dish, use butter and make your own. A trick I learned from one of Prue Leith's books, is to use semolina to mop up the juices and to stop the base pastry becoming soggy. *Serves 8-10*

1 × 2.3kg/5lb SALMON
500g/1lb PUFF PASTRY; DEFROSTED IF FROZEN
300g/10oz SKINNNED WHITE FISH FILLETS, SUCH AS LEMON SOLE, HADDOCK OR WHITING
2 (size 4) EGG WHITES
250ml/8fl oz DOUBLE CREAM
SALT AND PEPPER
10-15 TARRAGON LEAVES, CHOPPED
4-5 tbsp SEMOLINA
1 EGG, BEATEN

Preheat the oven to 230°C/450°F/gas 8. Roll out one piece of the pastry and using your template cut it into a fish shape. Put it on a wet baking sheet and prick it all over with a fork. Bake for 10 minutes, turn it over and bake for a further 5 minutes or until golden and crisp on both sides. Leave to cool and until needed.

If your fishmonger has not done it for you, fillet and skin the salmon and remove all other bones with a pair of tweezers. Measure the salmon fillets against the pastry. From each salmon fillet cut off a centre piece nearly the full length of the template, then cut the remaining pieces to fit down the sides. Cut off 125g/4oz of trimmings for the mousseline. Cut the white fish into cubes, and put it and the salmon trimmings into the fridge.

Following the instructions on page 86 and using the fish, egg whites and cream, make the mousseline, season it well and add the tarragon.

Put the pastry base flattest side downwards on a baking sheet, and dredge the semolina over it. Cover with a layer of salmon fillets and sprinkle with pepper. Salt draws the juices out from the salmon, so don't use it unless you plan to cook the fish immediately. Spread on the mousseline, cover with the remaining salmon and again sprinkle with a little pepper. Roll the remaining pastry out into a large sheet and being careful not to stretch it, lay over the top. Cut to shape, leaving a border of approximately 2.5cm/1 inch and, using a spatula to lift the edges, tuck the pastry in under the base.

From the pastry trimmings, cut two narrow crescents, one to mark off the head and the other for the mouth; a button for the eye, and some matchstick strips to make the tail. Add further fins if you like. Use beaten egg to stick these on to the fish, then mark the scales all down the body of the fish with a teaspoon. You can now cook the fish or keep it very cold in the fridge for a few hours.

To cook: heat the oven to 230°C/450°F/gas 8. Brush the fish all over with beaten egg and put into the oven, then after 15 minutes lower the temperature to 160°C/325°F/gas 3 and cook for a further 30 minutes. Before taking the fish from the oven, check that it is cooked by inserting a skewer: it should slide in very easily. Allow the fish to rest in a warm place for 5 minutes before cutting.

Serve with Beurre blanc sauce (page 50).

# Salmon en Croûte with an Asparagus Filling

This variation on the last recipe also makes an attractive summer dish; the mousseline that sandwiched the salmon together is replaced by an asparagus purée. *Serves 8-10.*

1 × 2.3kg/5lb SALMON
500g/1lb PUFF PASTRY, DEFROSTED IF FROZEN
750g-1kg/1½-2lb ASPARAGUS
75ml/3fl oz DOUBLE CREAM
1 tbsp CHOPPED DILL
SALT AND PEPPER
4-5 tbsp SEMOLINA
6 THIN RASHERS SWEET STREAKY BACON
1 EGG, BEATEN

Follow the previous recipe to prepare the template and the salmon, and to make and cook the base of the croûte.

To make the filling, cook the asparagus until tender. Put it in a blender or food processor, reduce to a purée, then add the cream and the dill, season well and, if you like a very smooth purée, push it all through a sieve.

Dredge the pastry base with semolina and lay the bacon rashers over it. Cover them with a layer of salmon, followed by a thick layer of the asparagus purée, then another layer of salmon and finally the remaining purée. Follow the instructions given in the last recipe to cover with pastry, to decorate and to cook.

Serve with a Hollandaise sauce (page 44)

# Stuffed Salmon

I love serving a stuffed fish as there is an element of surprise and a buzz of expecation as my guests wait to see what is inside.

The stuffing I give in the main recipe uses the unusual combination of mushrooms and broad beans. The variation that follows uses spinach and bacon. Both the stuffings are good with salmon and both add interest and colour to the dish.

The flavours are strong, so a robust sauce is needed. For the broad bean and mushroom stuffing, I suggest Béarnaise (page 47), flavoured with summer savory, sweet majoram or tarragon, and for the spinach stuffing tomato flavoured Béarnaise or Sauce Choron (page 49). *Serves 8-10.*

1 × 2.3-2.5kg/5-5½lb SALMON
1.5kg/3lb BROAD BEANS OR 340g/12oz PACKET FROZEN YOUNG BROAD BEANS
125ml/4fl oz MILK
125g/4oz BREADCRUMBS FROM A STALE LOAF
50g/2oz BUTTER
2 SHALLOTS, CHOPPED
250g/8oz MUSHROOMS, CHOPPED
2 EGGS
SALT AND PEPPER

Get your fishmonger to gut, remove the gills and bone the fish or follow the instructions on pages 20 and 24 and do it yourself.

Cook the broad beans, leave to cool and then, and this is tedious but well worthwhile, skin the beans. Use a knife to make a nick in the end and beans will easily pop out of the skin.

Pour the milk over the breadcrumbs and leave them to soak.

Melt the butter in a wide sauté pan or frying pan and cook the shallots until trans-parent. Add the mushrooms, raise the heat, and cook, stirring frequently, for around 10 minutes, or until the juices they release have evaporated.

Whisk the eggs, stir in the breadcrumbs, the broad beans and the mushrooms and sea-son well with salt and pepper.

Take a very large sheet of foil and brush with oil. Lay the salmon on it, and spoon in the stuffing. Reshape the fish around the stuffing and wrap it up tightly using the foil to keep the shape.

Put it on to a baking tray, curling it round if necessary, and cook in a preheated oven at 180°C/350°F/gas 4 for 12 minutes per 500g/1lb, using the weight of the fish after bon-ing, but before stuffing, as your guide.

Take the fish from the oven and let it rest for 10 minutes before unwrapping. Carefully skin the salmon, using the foil to turn it for the second side. Then, using the foil again, gently roll the fish on to a serving platter.

# Spinach and Bacon Stuffing

750g/1½lb FRESH SPINACH, OR 300g/10oz FROZEN SPINACH
125g/4oz BREADCRUMBS FROM A STALE LOAF
125ml/4fl oz MILK
1 tbsp OIL
1 ONION, CHOPPED
1 CLOVE GARLIC, CRUSHED
4-5 RASHERS STREAKY SWEET CURE BACON, CHOPPED
2 EGGS
1 tbsp LEMON JUICE
NUTMEG
SALT AND PEPPER

Use this as an alternative to the broad bean and mushroom stuffing above.

Cook the spinach, following the packet directions if frozen. Leave until cool, then squeeze dry and chop it.

Put the breadcrumbs in a bowl, pour over the milk and leave until needed.

In a frying pan heat the oil and sauté the onion and garlic until soft. Add the bacon and cook for a few minutes, or until it is soft and all the fat has been released. Remove the bacon and onion with a slotted spoon, and put to drain on a piece of kitchen paper.

In a large bowl whisk the eggs and lemon juice and season with a good grating of nutmeg and some salt and pepper. Stir in the spinach, breadcrumbs, bacon and onion and season further if necessary.

# The Memsahib's Sunday Lunch

The Memsahib, or the European wife living in India during the years of the British Raj, would have taught her servants to cook Western food, and a Sunday lunch party would have been the only occasion on which a full blown curry was served.

The Memsahib wouldn't have had a salmon, but, if her husband was the sporting type, he could have presented her with a mahseer, a large fish that comes from the rivers in the foothills of the Himalayas, and perhaps it would have arrived just in time for Sunday.

This recipe uses a whole salmon, which is boned, marinated with spices, stuffed with aromatic rice and eaten with a cooling raita. Indian or spiced vegetables are needed to complete the picture and I give, with a few changes, the recipe for Okra with onions and tomatoes in Sameen Rushdie's book *Indian Cookery*.

These amounts produce a medium curry, but if you like it hot use a second chilli in the marinade, and for a really fiery plateful, chop up yet another chilli and stir it into the raita. Conversely, you can tone it down by using less chilli and fewer spices.

This lunch serves 10-12 people.

# Rice-stuffed Salmon

*For the fish*
1 × 2.3-2.5kg/5-5½lb SALMON
1 CLOVE GARLIC, CRUSHED
2.5cm/1 inch PIECE GINGER, CHOPPED
1 GREEN CHILLI, VERY FINELY CHOPPED
1 tsp TURMERIC
½ tsp GROUND BLACK PEPPER
1 tbsp SUNFLOWER OIL

The salmon should be gutted and its gills removed, but there is no need to scale it. Follow the directions on page 24 to bone the salmon and keep the backbone and pieces for the stock.

In a pestle and mortar, or in a small mixing bowl and using a wooden spoon, combine the garlic, ginger, chilli, turmeric and pepper, and work in the oil to make a paste.

Take a very large sheet of foil, lay it on your work surface and smear all over with oil. Lay the salmon on it, open it up and lightly rub the spiced paste into the flesh. Close up the fish, wrap the foil loosely round it and leave it to marinate for 4-5 hours. Meanwhile, cook the rice for the stuffing.

*For the stuffing*
BONES OF THE SALMON
300g/10oz BASMATI RICE
2 MEDIUM ONIONS
5 CARDAMOM PODS
4 tbsp VEGETABLE OIL
SALT AND PEPPER
1 CLOVE GARLIC, FINELY CHOPPED
2.5cm/1 inch PIECE GINGER, FINELY CHOPPED
1 tsp CUMIN SEEDS
5cm/2 inch PIECE CINNAMON STICK
2 BAY LEAVES

Wash the rice thoroughly, put it in a large bowl of water, let it soak for 30 minutes then drain it and leave in a strainer to dry off for 15-20 minutes.

125

Put the salmon bones and one of the onions into a saucepan and pour in 750ml/1½ pints water. Bring to the boil, skim and simmer for 20 minutes. Drain off the stock and measure it. You will need 450ml/¾ pint. If necessary, reboil and reduce further.

Remove the seeds from the cardamom pods. Peel and slice the second onion, heat the oil in a heavy based pan, and cook the onion, stirring frequently, until it is golden brown. Add the rice, sprinkle with salt and a good grinding of pepper, and stir in the garlic, the ginger and the cardamom and cumin seeds. When the rice is glistening and well coated with oil, pour in the stock and stir, adding the cinnamon stick and the bayleaves. Bring to the boil, lower the heat, cover the pan very tightly and cook for 20 minutes. Remove the lid, check that the rice is cooked, and boil off any excess stock. Leave to cool.

Remove the cinnamon stick and bay leaves. Open the salmon and spoon the rice on to one side of it; there will seem to be a great deal and you may find you need to use the foil to keep it in. Finally, fold the foil over the salmon and secure it in a parcel.

Preheat the oven to 150°C/300°F/gas 2 and, using the original unboned weight of the salmon as your guide, cook it for 8 minutes per 500g/1lb. Take it from the oven and let it rest for 10 minutes, then carefully unwrap it and skin one side. Using the foil, turn the fish over and skin the other side. Use the foil again to help transfer the fish to a platter; in doing so you may find that some of the rice tumbles out, but use a spoon to tidy it up. If you wish, decorate the salmon with a little coriander or a few mint leaves, and serve it with a bowl of raita and the okra (below).

# *Raita*

1 LARGE CUCUMBER
SALT
450ml/¾ pint YOGHURT
JUICE OF ½ LEMON
375g/12oz TOMATOES, PEELED, DESEEDED AND CHOPPED
2 SPRING ONIONS, CHOPPED (OPTIONAL)

Peel the cucumber, shred it, sprinkle it with salt and leave to drain for an hour. Rinse the cucumber and pat it dry with kitchen paper. Pour the yoghurt into a bowl, whisk in the lemon juice then stir in the cucumber, tomato and, if using, the spring onion. Taste and add more salt and/or lemon juice, refrigerate and serve very cold.

# Okra with Onions and Tomatoes

Buy small tender, crisp okra, cook them this way and thoughts of an overboiled sticky mess will disappear for ever. This dish can be made ahead and reheated gently just before needed.

1kg/2lb OKRA
8 tbsp SUNFLOWER OIL
1 ONION, PEELED AND SLICED INTO THIN RINGS OR HALF RINGS
1 tsp MUSTARD SEEDS
3-4 GARLIC CLOVES, PEELED AND CRUSHED
3.5cm/1½ inch PIECE GINGER, FINELY CHOPPED
1 tsp TURMERIC
1 tsp RED CHILLI POWDER (OR TO TASTE)
1 tsp GROUND CORIANDER
SALT
375g/12oz TOMATOES, PEELED, DESEEDED AND ROUGHLY CHOPPED

Wash and dry the okra, top and tail them and cut them into 2.5-3.5cm/1-1½ inch pieces.

In a wok or large frying pan, heat the oil and fry the onion until golden brown. Then add the mustard seeds followed by the garlic, ginger, turmeric, red chilli powder, coriander and a teaspoon of salt. Stir-fry for a minute or two, add the okra and mix it well with the spices. Cover, lower the heat, and cook for 5 minutes. Add the tomatoes, replace the cover and cook, checking once or twice to make sure it isn't burning, for a further 10-15 minutes, or until the okra are tender.

# Stir-fried Vegetables with Steamed Salmon

China does not abound with salmon rivers, but if it did, Chinese cuisine would surely abound with salmon recipes. This recipe, which isn't as complicated as it might look, uses two Chinese techniques: steaming and stir-frying. In authentic Chinese cuisine these would not be combined in the same dish; in East meets West cuisine I think it perfectly acceptable to do so.

The selection of vegetables given here blends nicely with the fish, but others would be just as good, as long as you choose different colours and textures.

The use of the two techniques means that the fish and the vegetables need to be cooked separately in the wok. The best way of doing this is to prepare and blanch the vegetables, steam the fish and then finally stir-fry the vegetables.

*To blanch the vegetables*
125g/4oz CARROTS
125g/4oz MUSHROOMS
125g/4oz CUCUMBER
250g/8oz FRESH BEANSPROUTS
SALT

Start by preparing the vegetables. Peel the carrots and cut them into thin diagonal slices. Wipe the mushrooms, cut the stalks flush with the caps, discard them and slice the mushrooms. Peel and cut the cucumber into 2.5-3.5cm/1-1½ inch chunks and cut these lengthwise into quarters. Discard the seeds, then cut into matchstick pieces. Wash the beansprouts and leave to drain.

The prepared vegetables now need to be blanched and, if you do this in advance you can use your wok; otherwise use a saucepan. Half fill your wok or saucepan with water, add salt and bring it to a rolling boil. Put in the carrots; after 30 seconds add the mushrooms and cucumber, and after another 30 seconds the beansprouts, leaving them for only 15 seconds. Drain the vegetables and immediately plunge them into a bowl of cold water to arrest the cooking and preserve the colours.

*To steam the salmon*
MIDDLE-CUT SALMON APPROXIMATELY 625g/1¼lb, OR TAILPIECE
APPROXIMATELY 750g/1½lb
1 tbsp FINELY CHOPPED FRESH GINGER

When you are ready to cook the salmon pour about 5cm/2 inches water into the wok, set the trivet over it and bring to the boil. Place the fish in a shallow dish that will fit on top of the trivet and sprinkle the ginger over the top.

Put the dish on the trivet, lower the heat to keep the water at a simmer, and put on the lid. The fish will cook in about 15 minutes, depending on its thickness and the amount of steam, but as it is going to be kept warm, it should be slightly undercooked. When the fish is ready, remove the dish from the wok and cover it to keep warm.

*To stir-fry the vegetables*
2 tbsp VEGETABLE OIL
5mm/¼ inch PIECE FRESH GINGER, CUT INTO MATCHSTICKS
1-2 SPRING ONIONS, CHOPPED
SMALL HANDFUL CHOPPED CORIANDER
1-2 tsp SOY SAUCE
SALT

Rinse out the wok, dry it and put over a high heat. Add the oil and the ginger, and when the oil starts to smoke, all the blanched vegetables. Stir-fry them, tossing and turning all the time for about 2 minutes, or until just tender. Halfway through the cooking add the spring onions, and at the end the coriander, the soy sauce and a sprinkling of salt. Turn the vegetables into a warm serving dish.

*To finish*
1 tbsp SESAME OIL
1 tbsp VEGETABLE OIL
1 SPRING ONION, FINELY CHOPPED
1 tbsp LIGHT SOY SAUCE

In a small pan heat the oils until they start to smoke. Place the fish on top of the vegetables, sprinkle the spring onion and soy sauce over it and finally pour on the sizzling oil.

# PIES, PASTA AND OTHER DISHES

Salmon is a good addition to fish pies, pasta or to a large variety of made-up dishes. The recipes are useful as most of them need only a comparatively small amount of salmon, and frequently leftover cooked fish may be used.

During the writing of this book, many people said to me: 'I do hope you are going to include fish cakes and kedgeree.' My answer is to offer them here. Some of the other recipes may be less familiar, but they are all worth while.

## *Fish Pie*

The addition of mayonnaise may be unconventional but it adds a new lively dimension to a basic fish pie.

75g/3oz BUTTER
1 CLOVE GARLIC
150ml/¼ pint MAYONNAISE
450ml/¾ pint MILK
½ ONION
250g/8oz WHITE FISH FILLETS
250g/8oz SALMON
125g/4oz PRAWNS, DEFROSTED IF FROZEN
25g/1oz FLOUR
SHREDDED BASIL
250g/8oz TOMATOES, PEELED, DESEEDED AND ROUGHLY CHOPPED
SALT AND PEPPER
750g/1½lb POTATOES, COOKED AND MASHED WITH BUTTER AND MILK
2 tbsp BREADCRUMBS

Squeeze the garlic clove through a garlic press and stir it into the mayonnaise.

Pour the milk into a wide pan, add the onion and put to heat. When it is nearly at boiling point, add the white fish and simmer for 5 minutes or until just done. Remove the fish, replace with the salmon and cook for a further 5 minutes. Flake both lots of fish and put it into a bowl with the prawns.

Melt half the butter, stir in the flour, slowly add the strained milk and cook until thick and smooth. Take from the heat, leave to cool slightly then stir in the mayonnaise, the basil and the tomatoes, season well with salt and pepper and fold in the fish. Spoon the mixture into the pie dish. Cover with the mashed potato, sprinkle with the bread-crumbs, dot with the remaining butter and bake immediately at 190°C/375°F/gas 5 for 25 minutes or until the top is brown.

# Parcels of Salmon, Potato and Olive Oil

Potatoes, salmon and fruity olive oil wrapped up in foil parcels. This is best eaten warm rather than straight from the oven, or as the French would say, *tiède*.

These foil parcels make good picnic food; they eliminate the need for lots of dishes, as all each picnicker needs is a parcel, a plate and a fork. After cooking the parcels, wrap them in several tea towels, or put them into an insulated bag, and they should remain warm for some time.

4 SALMON STEAKS OR PIECES FILLET, OR A TAILPIECE
250g/8oz NEW OR WAXY POTATOES, DICED
2 SHALLOTS, FINELY CHOPPED
SMALL BUNCH CHIVES, CHOPPED
5 tbsp OLIVE OIL
SALT AND PEPPER

Using a plate as a guide cut 8 circles of foil with a diameter of approximately 23cm/9 inches.

Boil the potatoes in salted water until just soft. Mix them with the shallots, half the chives, 3 tbsp olive oil, and season well.

Bone and skin the salmon and cut it into cubes. Brush the inside of four of the foil circles with a little oil and divide the potato mixture up between them. Place the salmon cubes on top, sprinkle with salt, pepper and the remaining chives and drizzle with oil.

Cover each circle with another piece of foil and double fold round the edge to seal each parcel. Cook in a preheated oven at 190°C/375°F/gas 5 for 8 minutes.

An alternative is to use silicone or greaseproof paper and cook the parcels in a micro-wave. They will take 5 minutes.

# Filo Pie with Salmon and Jerusalem Artichokes

Filo pastry for a pie is best baked in a flat based metal dish, as only metal will generate enough heat to cook the bottom layer of pastry properly. You will need a dish with a diameter of 18-20cm/7-8 inches. A paella dish is ideal but you could use a flan dish, a cake tin or, if it will fit into your oven, a frying pan.

When arranging the pastry over the top of the pie, try not to let the sheets stick together and become thick and heavy. Lift them up individually so that the top of the cooked pie will resemble layers of crisp tissue paper.

375g/12oz JERUSALEM ARTICHOKES
375-500g/12oz-1lb SALMON STEAKS OR FILLET, OR 375g/12oz COOKED SALMON,
FLAKED
350ml/12fl oz MILK
BAY LEAF AND A FEW PARSLEY STALKS
SALT AND PEPPER
50ml/2fl oz WHITE WINE
40g/1½oz BUTTER
40g/1½oz FLOUR
2 tbsp DOUBLE CREAM
1 tbsp CHOPPED PARSLEY
75g/3oz BUTTER FOR THE PASTRY
4 LARGE OR 6-8 SMALL SHEETS FILO PASTRY

Top, tail, peel and slice the artichokes. You will probably end up with 225-250g/7-8oz, depending on how knobbly they are. Heat the milk with the bay leaf, parsley stalks, 2 or 3 peppercorns and some salt, in a frying pan or small sauté pan. Add the artichokes and simmer them for 15 minutes or until tender. Remove the artichokes with a slotted spoon.

If you are using fresh salmon, poach it in the same milk until just cooked. Remove to a plate and skin, bone and flake it.

Strain the milk into a jug and add the wine to it. Don't worry if it curdles as it will homogenize when it is stirred into the roux. In a clean saucepan melt the butter, stir in the flour and after it has cooked for a minute or two, slowly add the milk mixture, stirring until you have a smooth thick sauce. Take it from the heat, stir in the cream and chopped parsley and check the seasoning. Gently stir in the artichoke slices and the salmon.

Place a baking sheet in the centre of the oven and preheat it 180°C/350°F/gas 4.

Melt the butter for the pastry and brush some round the cooking pan. Unroll the filo sheets and cover with a damp cloth. Remove them one at a time, cut them in half, brush with butter, fold over and brush both sides with butter. Arrange 6 pieces (3 sheets) in the pan to cover the base and extend at an angle like flower petals over the edge. Spoon the salmon and artichoke into the centre and fold the extending petals over it. Cut the final sheet of filo into four, butter it, and arrange it in folds over the top.

Place on the hot baking sheet and bake for 30-35 minutes or until golden brown.


# Baklava of Spinach and Salmon

This looks very similar to the famous Greek sweet, but the filling of nuts and sugar syrup is abandoned in favour of spinach and salmon.

I find this recipe really useful as it is equally good hot, warm or tepid, and can be left on the side until needed. It also makes good picnic food.

250g/8oz COOKED SALMON, FLAKED
750g/1½lb FRESH SPINACH OR 300g/10oz FROZEN SPINACH
125g/4oz BUTTER
25g/1oz FLOUR
150ml/¼ pint MILK
NUTMEG
SALT AND PEPPER
4 LARGE OR 6-8 SMALL SHEETS FILO PASTRY

If using fresh spinach, lightly cook and leave to drain. If using frozen, open the packet, turn it into a sieve and leave until defrosted.

Make a thick white sauce with 25g/1oz butter, the flour and milk. Stir in the spinach and the flaked salmon and season with grated nutmeg, salt and pepper.

Grease a 19cm/7 inch square cake or baking tin. Melt the remaining butter in a small saucepan. Unwrap the pastry and, to stop it drying out, cover with a damp cloth. Take a sheet at a time: brush it all over with melted butter and fold, as many times as necessary, brushing each surface with butter, until it is the same size as the tin. Place in the tin and continue until you have used half the pastry.

Spoon in the salmon and spinach mixture, smooth over the top and, in just the same way, cover with the remaining pastry.

Brush butter generously over the top and then, using a sharp knife, cut the pastry crosswise from corner to corner. Make further diagonal cuts across each side to make lozenge shapes; be sure to cut right through to the bottom.

Heat the oven to 180°C/350°F/gas 4 and bake for 25 minutes, then turn the oven down to 150°C/300°F/gas 2. Bake for a further 15 minutes or until everything is bubbling and the top is crisp and brown.

# Carrot, Calabrese and Salmon Flan

If you have some leftover salmon, this flan makes a complete lunch or quick meal. The cheese pastry is delicious, but in a hurry, you could roll out a packet of frozen shortcrust.

*For the pastry*
175g/6oz PLAIN FLOUR
½ tsp MUSTARD POWDER
SALT AND CAYENNE PEPPER
75g/3oz BUTTER
125g/4oz CHEDDAR CHEESE, GRATED
1 EGG YOLK

Mix together the flour, mustard and seasonings, rub in the butter and mix in the cheese. Add the egg yolk, and mix to obtain a dough; you may need to add a few drops of cold water.

If making the pastry in a food processor start by fitting the grating disc and grating the cheese into the bowl. Change to the double-bladed knife, add the flour, seasonings and butter, cut into cubes. Process until the mixture resembles fine breadcrumbs then, through the feed tube, add the egg yolk and continue processing, adding a few drops of water if necessary, until the pastry is formed and balls round the central column.

Wrap the pastry in foil, put it to relax in the fridge for 20 minutes, then roll it out and use to line a 25cm/10 inch flan tin. Prick the base with a fork, cover with a piece of foil and weigh it down with beans or rice in the centre. Preheat the oven to 190°C/375°F/gas 5, put the prepared flan on a baking sheet and cook for 10-12 minutes. Remove the foil and return the flan to the oven for a further 5-7 minutes or until the pastry is golden.

*For the filling*
300-375g/10-12oz COOKED SALMON, FLAKED
125g/4oz CARROTS, CUT INTO BATONS
1 HEAD CALABRESE, CUT INTO FLORETS
450ml/¾ pint MILK
1 SLICE ONION
1 BAY LEAF
6 PEPPERCORNS
A FEW PARSLEY STALKS
40g/1½oz BUTTER
40g/1½oz FLOUR
SALT AND PEPPER

Pour the milk into a pan, add the onion, bayleaf, peppercorns and parsley stalks, bring it to the boil, then remove from the heat and leave to infuse for 15 minutes.

Cook the carrots and calabrese by any method you like: boiling, steaming or microwaving. Set aside until needed.

Make a béchamel sauce with the butter, flour and milk and season it with salt and pepper.

Put the salmon in bottom of the prepared pastry case, arrange the carrots and calabrese over it, then pour on the béchamel, making sure that the vegetables are covered. Heat the oven to 180°C/360°F/gas 4, cover the flan with foil and cook through for 10-15 minutes.

# Quiche of Salmon and Mushrooms

A good basic quiche with a tasty filling.

You will need to make and bake blind a 30cm/10 inch pastry case. Use shortcrust pastry made with 250g/8oz flour.

250g/8oz COOKED SALMON
125g/4oz MUSHROOMS, CHOPPED
25g/1oz BUTTER
3 EGGS
150ml/¼ pint FROMAGE BLANC OR SINGLE CREAM
1 tsp TOMATO PURÉE
SALT AND PEPPER

In a frying pan melt the butter and cook the mushrooms, stirring constantly, until the juices run. Remove the pan from the heat and keep until needed.

Put the salmon, the eggs, the fromage blanc or cream, the tomato purée and seasonings into a food processor or blender and process until smooth. Add the mushrooms and their liquid and process briefly to mix them in.

Put the mixture into the prepared flan and bake in a preheated oven at 190°C/375°F/gas 5 for 20-25 minutes or until the filling has set.

# Curry Puffs

These puffs make good snack food, as I discovered when I left some on the side in my kitchen, to find the next morning that they had all disappeared.

175g/6oz SALMON, SKINNED AND BONED
50g/2oz BLANCHED FLAKED ALMONDS
2 tbsp VEGETABLE OIL
1 MEDIUM SPANISH ONION, THINLY SLICED
1cm/½ inch GINGER, FINELY CHOPPED
½ tsp GARAM MASALA
25g/1oz RAISINS
SALT
250g/8oz FROZEN PUFF PASTRY, THAWED
1 EGG

Brown the almonds under the grill or by putting them in a hot oven for a few minutes.

In a frying pan heat the oil and gently fry the onion and the ginger. When the onion is soft and transparent stir in the garam masala, raisins and almonds and season with a little salt. Take the pan from the heat and leave to cool.

Cut the salmon into cubes of about the size of the end of your little finger and stir them into the cooled curry mixture.

Roll out the pastry into a square of about 30cm/12 inches and cut it into four 15cm/6 inch squares. Spoon a quarter of the filling on to one half of each square. Dampen all round the edge with a little water, turn over corner to corner to make triangles, and seal the edges. Brush the tops with a little beaten egg and bake in a preheated oven at 220°C/425°F/gas 7 for 20-25 minutes or until golden.

# Lasagne with Fennel and Salmon

Lasagne is a food for family and close friends, and is at its best eaten cheerfully, along with a salad and vino da casa, round the kitchen table. Salmon and fennel are well disposed towards each other and the use of soured cream or crème fraîche adds sharpness and lightness to the dish.

Make the lasagne with fresh pasta, homemade or bought, which needs only light cooking and draining before you layer it in the dish. If you use packet lasagne of the 'no pre-cook' variety, keep the sauces very wet as the sheets soak up a great deal of liquid.

Bought lasagne comes in a variety of sizes; if possible, use a dish that comfortably takes two sheets side by side, otherwise break them to size and use an extra one if there is a margin that needs filling.

Lasagne is very accommodating; it can be made up to two days ahead and kept re-frigerated, and it can also be kept warm for up to an hour after cooking.

6 SHEETS LASAGNE
250g/8oz COOKED SALMON, FLAKED
375g/12oz FENNEL
75g/3oz BUTTER
1 tbsp OIL
1 SMALL ONION, FINELY CHOPPED
1 SMALL CLOVE GARLIC, CRUSHED
2 tbsp WHITE WINE (OPTIONAL)
600ml/1 pint MILK
1 tsp FENUGREEK SEEDS
25g/1oz FLOUR
SALT AND PEPPER
150ml/¼ pint SOURED CREAM OR CRÈME FRAÎCHE

Remove any outer leaves and feathery pieces from the fennel and cut it into thin slices.

Heat just under half the butter with the oil in a frying pan or sauté pan and fry the onion with the garlic until transparent. Add the fennel, continue frying until slightly softened, then pour in 125ml/4fl oz water and, if you are using it, the wine. Leave it cooking over a low heat, stirring occasionally and adding extra water if necessary, for about 20 minutes or until the fennel is soft and the liquid has much reduced. Remove from the stove and keep until needed.

Meanwhile make a béchamel sauce. Pour the milk in a pan, add the fenugreek seeds, bring to nearly boiling point, then take from the heat. Melt the remaining butter, stir in the flour, and cook for a minute or so before slowly adding the milk and the fenugreek. Stir constantly until the sauce is thick and smooth, season well and let it simmer for a few minutes before removing it from the heat.

Mix the salmon with half the béchamel and, if it seems at all stiff, stir in further milk. Mix the soured cream or crème fraîche into the other half and adjust the seasoning.

Butter an ovenproof dish and then build up the lasagne. Smear a couple of table-spoons of the béchamel over the bottom of the dish, cover with a layer of pasta followed by the fennel, then more pasta, the salmon and a final layer of lasagne. Top it all with the béchamel.

Cover the lasagne with a piece of foil and cook at 180°C/350°F/gas 4 for 50-60 minutes, removing the foil halfway through to let the top lightly brown.

# Anellini Farciti

Anellini are little pasta rings, stuffed, turned over into a half moon shape and sealed. You will have to make the pasta yourself, but it is not difficult. No bought pasta sheets are thin enough; if you use them, you will have a heavy and stodgy meal.

The filling and the pesto-based sauce are simple to prepare. Make the sauce with the best quality fruity olive oil and a fresh block of parmigiano grano, and every moment spent making the anellini will be worthwhile. *Serves 4 as a main course or 6 as a first course.*

*For the pasta*
300g/10oz PLAIN FLOUR
3 EGGS

The easiest way to make pasta dough is in a food processor, but otherwise make it by mixing the flour and eggs and kneading until you have a smooth and elastic dough. If you are using a food processor, put in the flour and eggs, process until they have formed a ball round the central column and then continue to process for a further minute to knead the dough. Divide the dough into four, roll into balls and, to stop the pasta drying out, wrap each one separately in foil. Leave to rest while you make the stuffing.

*For the stuffing*
125g/4oz SALMON, SKINNED AND BONED
125g/4oz RICOTTA
1 EGG YOLK
A FEW LEAVES BASIL
SALT AND PEPPER

Cut the salmon into pieces and put it and all the other ingredients into a food processor. Process until smooth.

Roll out the pasta one piece at a time, and cut out and fill each sheet before you start on the next one. If you have a pasta roller, put the dough through that until you reach the thinnest setting, but if you don't, use a rolling pin, and work quickly or the pasta will dry out and crack. Always roll away from you, turning the pasta sheet or *sfoglia* a little between each movement and continuing until the sheet is very thin and feels like a piece of chamois leather when you run your fingers over it.

Cut out the pasta with a 6cm/2½ inch biscuit cutter and place a small mound of the filling on one half. Brush round the edge with a little water, fold over the dough and seal it, either by pressing round the edge with the prongs of a fork or, less authentic but quicker, running a pastry wheel round it. Continue with the other sheets of pasta and put the finished anellini on a rack to dry; you will have 50-60.

As the anellini are stuffed with fresh fish they should be cooked very quickly, but they do freeze well and can then be cooked from frozen. If freezing, stop them sticking together by sprinkling lightly with flour before packing them in plastic bags.

Cook the anellini in plenty of boiling well salted water. If fresh they will take 15-18 minutes, and if frozen about 5 minutes longer.

*For the sauce*
75ml/3fl oz OLIVE OIL
1 CLOVE GARLIC, CRUSHED
2 tbsp PINENUTS
A HANDFUL BASIL LEAVES
A LITTLE PARMESAN
SALT AND PEPPER

While the pasta is cooking, prepare the sauce. Put the olive oil and garlic in a small saucepan and warm over a low heat. In a dry frying pan, toast the pinenuts until golden.

Drain the anellini, but not too well, and put them on hot plates. Discard the garlic, dribble the warm olive oil over the anellini and sprinkle with the pinenuts and some torn basil leaves. Using a grater, shred a little parmesan over the top and finish with a good grinding of pepper.

# Pasta with a Dolcelatte and Salmon Sauce

This recipe, with its lovely creamy sauce, qualifies for an entry in the 'Cooked in 10 Minutes' list and is best made with pasta shapes of the type that hold a sauce well. They have such lovely names: conchiglie (shells) or farfalle (butterflies) are both suitable. *Serves 4 as a main course or 6 as a first course.*

450g/14oz DRIED PASTA SHAPES
250g/8oz SALMON, SKINNED AND BONED
300ml/½ pint SINGLE CREAM
3-4 SAGE LEAVES, CHOPPED
125g/4oz DOLCELATTE
SALT AND PEPPER

Bring a large pan of water to the boil, salt it, add the pasta and cook following the directions on the packet.

Meanwhile, put the cream in a bowl and stand it over a pan of simmering water. Cut the salmon and the cheese into pieces and add them, along with the sage, to the cream. Stirring occasionally, let it heat for 7-8 minutes, or until the salmon is cooked and the dolcelatte melted, then season with salt and pepper.

Drain the pasta, tip it into a serving dish, pour over the cream sauce and toss it well.

# Kedgeree

I well remember as a child munching my way through a plate of what I thought was delicious kedgeree while listening to the grown-ups talking nostalgically about kedgeree made with salmon. A kedgeree made with large flakes of smoked haddock, a few fried onions and a little curry powder is one of the great dishes from the British Raj; kedgeree made with salmon has an entirely different character. It should be gentle and soothing and is much better very lightly spiced or not spiced at all. The other point to consider is whether it should be dry or creamy; when made with salmon, I prefer it creamy, but if you like it dry just leave out the final addition of egg and cream.

If you want to eat it cold, mix the newly cooked rice, fish and hardboiled eggs together, moistening the mixture with a little of the poaching liquid or some cream, and then just before serving, stir in a couple of tablespoons of mayonnaise, chopped parsley and some snipped chives. For a party the chopped hardboiled eggs can be replaced by a few whole quails eggs.

250g/8oz COOKED SALMON, FLAKED
225g/7oz BASMATI OR LONG-GRAIN RICE
3 HARDBOILED EGGS, CHOPPED
50g/2oz BUTTER
1 tbsp CHOPPED PARSLEY
SALT AND PEPPER
1 EGG
150ml/¼ pint DOUBLE CREAM

Cook the rice, then drain it under a hot tap to make sure that the grains are separated. In a saucepan, melt the butter, add the salmon, rice, hardboiled eggs, parsley and the seasonings, and cook gently, stirring occasionally, trying not to break up the salmon flakes, until the kedgeree is hot. If you start with cold rice, salmon and eggs you may find that it is best to heat them by putting them in a bowl, covering it, and placing it over a pan of simmering water for about 20 minutes.

Serve when it is hot or, for the creamy version, whisk the egg and cream together, stir them into the hot kedgeree and cook for a further 2 minutes.

# Fritters

Delicious crisp morsels. Serve just as they are, with the light herb sauce on page 63, or with a few drops of soy sauce.

250g/8oz COOKED SALMON, FLAKED
50g/2oz FLOUR
2 EGGS
150ml/¼ pint MILK OR THIN CREAM
SALT AND PEPPER
OIL AND BUTTER FOR FRYING

Make a thick batter by mixing together the flour, eggs, and milk or cream, and season with salt and pepper. Stir in the salmon, and leave to stand for half an hour or so.

In a frying pan heat some oil and butter – about two-thirds oil to one third butter – to a depth of 5mm-1cm/¼-½ inch.

Drop in spoonfuls of the batter, fry for a minute or so or until brown, then turn the fritters over with a spatula and fry until the other side is also brown and crisp. Drain on kitchen paper.

# Potato and Salmon Gratin

This is based on the French Gratin Dauphinois and, although best made with fresh salmon, it is a good way of using up cooked fish. The exact weight is not crucial; use what you have, a little bit more or less will do no harm.

If you have a very hungry family you could increase the amount of potatoes, but remember that you will then need to add a little more cream or milk.

500g/1lb POTATOES
375g/12oz SALMON, FRESH OR COOKED
A LITTLE BUTTER
1 SMALL ONION, CHOPPED
1 tbsp CHOPPED DILL
SALT AND PEPPER
300ml/½ pint SINGLE CREAM, OR HALF CREAM AND HALF MILK
1 EGG

Boil the potatoes until barely cooked. Drain, and when cool, peel and slice them.

If the salmon is fresh, cut it into thin strips; if cooked, flake it.

Butter a deep ovenproof dish. Put a layer of potatoes on the bottom, cover them with a layer of salmon and then sprinkle on some onion, dill and pepper. Continue with the layers until everything is used up; make sure to finish with potatoes.

Whisk the cream, eggs and some salt together and pour it over the top. Use a fork to make sure that it sinks down the sides.

Cook at 180°C/350°F/gas 4 for 30 minutes or until the top is golden.

# Fish Cakes

Fish cakes were part of the repetoire of the good plain English cook and were much eaten in wartime in ration-starved Britain. It is salutary to read Philip Harben in his 1945 book *The Way to Cook*.

> A useful proportion is one part of fish to two of potatoes. Some cooks boast that they can use a much smaller proportion of fish than this and still produce a good fish cake; it is perfectly true that even as much as ten parts of potato to one part of fish will produce something that is actually recognizable as a fish cake, but it is very far from being good.

Nowadays we make fish cakes with equal amounts of fish and potato and sometimes, but then the whole point of fish cakes starts to get lost, we reverse Philip Harben's 'useful proportion' and use two parts of fish to one of potatoes. Anyway, fish cakes should be kept plain, and do not, to my mind, need too many spices, flavourings or fashionable herbs, but they should not be made with stale leftovers; the potato should be freshly mashed and the fish newly cooked. They are best simply served with grilled tomatoes or accompanied by a little béchamel sauce with a few lightly cooked mushrooms or a chopped hardboiled egg stirred into it.

This mixture should make about eight large fish cakes, or many more tiny ones to be eaten at drinks time, speared with toothpicks and accompanied by mayonnaise for dipping.

300g/10oz COOKED SALMON, FLAKED
300g/10oz COOKED POTATO, MASHED WITH 25g/1oz BUTTER
2 tbsp PARSLEY, CHOPPED
½ SAGE LEAF, CHOPPED, OR PINCH DRIED SAGE
SHAKE ANCHOVY ESSENCE, IF LIKED
SALT AND PEPPER
1 EGG

*For the coating*
1 EGG
FLOUR
FRESH WHITE BREADCRUMBS
OIL OR HALF AND HALF OIL AND BUTTER FOR FRYING

Mix together the fish, potato, herbs and seasonings; if both the fish and potato are cold, you will find it easier to combine them if you heat them gently in a bowl set over a pan of simmering water. Lightly beat the egg, stir it in and check the seasoning. Spread the mixture out on to a piece of silicone paper or oiled foil and chill in the fridge for at least 2 hours.

When you are ready to cook, break the egg for the coating on to a plate and lightly beat it. Spread the flour over a second plate, and the breadcrumbs over a third. Shape the mixture into fish cakes, and dip them first into the flour, then into the egg and finally into the breadcrumbs. Heat about 5mm/¼ inch oil, or oil and butter mixed, in a pan and fry the fish cakes for about 3 minutes each side or until they are hot right through and golden and crisp on the outside.

# Croquettes

Croquettes appeared frequently in cookery books of the 1930s, when they were often re-ferred to as nursery food. They often incorporated leftovers from the adults' lunch table, and the contrast between the crisp-fried coating and the soft inside had particular appeal for children.

In this book I have kept fried food to a minimum, but as these croquettes are one of the very best ways of using up cold salmon, I think it would be sad not to include the recipe. If you have any extra parsley, deep-fry the sprigs and garnish the croquettes with them.

In a hurry you can use packet breadcrumbs, but they are much better made at home. Use a food processor to reduce 3 or 4 slices of bread to crumbs, place the crumbs on a bak-ing tray and bake in a medium oven, watching them and turning frequently, for 20-30 minutes or until they are golden. Put them back into the food processor and process until they are fine and crisp. Store any unused crumbs in an airtight jar.

250g/8oz COLD SALMON, FLAKED
40g/1½oz BUTTER
1 SHALLOT, VERY FINELY CHOPPED
40g/1½oz FLOUR
300ml/½ pint MILK
2 tbsp DOUBLE CREAM (OPTIONAL)
2 tbsp CHOPPED PARSLEY
SALT AND PEPPER
1 EGG, BEATEN
FLOUR AND BREADCRUMBS
OIL FOR FRYING

Melt the butter, add the shallot and cook gently until it has softened. Stir in the flour, then the milk, and when it has all been incorporated and the sauce is smooth, take the pan from the heat.

If you are using it, stir in the cream. Add the parsley, season to taste and gently stir in the salmon. Spoon the mixture on to a sheet of silicone paper and put flat in the refrig-erator. Leave until it is cold and firm.

Make the croquettes – this quantity should make 8. Wet your hands, shape the mix-ture, then roll each one in flour, then in beaten egg and finally in breadcrumbs. Fry in deep fat, or in a pan with 2.5cm/1 inch hot oil, turning the croquettes once. Drain on kitchen paper and eat while hot.

Crêpes with dill and smoked salmon

# Tortilla

Tortillas or Spanish omelettes have always featured in our household. My parents used to live in Spain and when my children were small they spent a lot of time there, and on their return always demanded tortillas. I became equally addicted and took to adding extra vegetables, chorizo or leftovers to the basic tortilla ingredients. My children weren't brought up on salmon tortillas, but if the speedy disappearance of one I made is anything to go by, they wouldn't have minded if they had been.

In Spain a tortilla is made in a well used and seasoned steel frying pan, but I admit to cheating and using a nonstick one. If you do use anything else follow the instructions about wiping it out very carefully or you will land up with a stuck soggy mess.

2 MEDIUM POTATOES, PEELED AND SLICED
200ml/7fl oz SUNFLOWER OIL OR MIXED OLIVE AND SUNFLOWER OIL
½ SMALL SPANISH ONION, SLICED
4 EGGS
SALT AND PEPPER
250g/8oz SALMON, SKINNED, BONED AND FLAKED

Heat the oil in a 20-22cm/8-9 inch frying pan and slide in the potato slices one at a time to stop them from sticking together. Layer the potato and onion and cook gently, turning occasionally, until soft but not brown.

Meanwhile, in a large bowl beat the eggs and season with salt and pepper. Remove the potatoes and onions from the pan with a slotted spoon and drain off as much oil as you can, then add them to the eggs. Press the potatoes down until they are covered by the egg, but try not to break up the slices. Leave them for 15 to 20 minutes.

Pour the oil into a bowl and reserve. Wipe out the pan, removing any stuck particles, then put it back on the heat and pour in 2 tbsp of the reserved oil. When it is very hot, spoon in and spread out half the egg and potato mixture, cover it with the salmon, and spoon the remaining egg and potato on the top. Turn the heat down and cook, shaking the pan frequently to avoid sticking, until the bottom is golden. Slide the tortilla on to a large plate, add a further tablespoon of oil to the pan and return the tortilla uncooked side downwards. When the bottom has set, finish cooking the tortilla by turning it two or three more times and cooking briefly on each side. When it has browned on both sides turn it on to a plate and leave to cool.

The tortilla should still be moist in the centre. It is best if left to cool and eaten at room temperature.

Tagliatelle with smoked salmon

# Stuffed Cabbage

*Chou farci* is much eaten in France and is normally stuffed with leftover meat combined with chopped sausage. However, the French have also discovered that salmon is good with cabbage, and used as here to stuff one, it makes a dish that needs little last minute attention.

I like to make this using a savoy cabbage, but primo is also suitable. For a party you could replace the large cabbage with the small individual ones that are now available.

If you have a big deep steamer, cook the cabbage in that; you will find that it will cook evenly and keep its shape well. Otherwise, use a deep saucepan with a close fitting lid and not too much water. The timings will remain the same.

To keep the stuffing in, the tradition in France is to tie up and cook the cabbage in a string bag. Nowadays few of us have spare string bags, so I use two new J-cloths (not pink ones as the colour runs) and find that they work very well.

1.5-1.8kg/3-3½lb CABBAGE
75g/3oz LONG-GRAIN RICE
375g/12oz SALMON, SKINNED AND BONED
1-2 tsp CHOPPED DILL OR THYME
SALT AND PEPPER

*For the sauce*
25g/1oz BUTTER
25g/1oz FLOUR
DILL OR THYME
SALT AND PEPPER

Remove any muddy or torn outside leaves from the cabbage and cut the bottom flush with the remaining leaves. Either steam the cabbage or cook in a saucepan of simmering water, with the lid on. A savoy needs 20 minutes and a tight-hearted primo 25. Remove the cabbage and leave until cool. Reserve the cooking water to make the sauce.

Following the directions on the package cook the rice, then turn it into a sieve and rinse it well under running tap.

When the cabbage has cooled, carefully peel back three or four layers of outside leaves and, using a sharp knife, cut out the heart, making sure to leave enough stalk at the bottom to hold the stuffing in. Cut off and discard any stalk or hard pieces attached to the heart, roughly chop the remainder and keep until needed.

Cut the salmon into bite sized cubes and combine them with the rice in a large bowl. Add enough chopped cabbage to make a good mix without overwhelming the fish. Sprinkle in the dill or thyme and season generously with salt and pepper.

Lay out the J-cloths across each other on a flat surface. Put the cabbage in the middle and spoon the stuffing into the centre. Fold over the leaves and then use the J-cloths to wrap it into a secure parcel.

Steam, or simmer in a deep saucepan without too much water, for 2 hours.

For the sauce, make a roux with the butter and flour and stir in about 450ml/¾ pint of the initial cooking liquid (or cooking liquid and water or milk), or as much as is needed to give a good consistency. Add a little dill or thyme, season to taste and let it bubble for 10 minutes before serving.

Take the cabbage from the steamer or saucepan, unwrap the cloths and reverse the cabbage on to a large plate. Reverse it again to get it the right way up on a serving dish.

Cut and serve the cabbage like a Christmas pudding and hand the sauce separately.

# Scrambled Eggs Rosebery

Nancy Shaw in *Food for the Greedy* gives Lord Cobham as the source of this recipe. The dish is simple: scramble some eggs, mix in some remains of cold salmon, and add salt and pepper. Lord Cobham says: 'If properly made, this dish should reproduce Lord Rosebery's racing colours: viz., primrose and rose. It looks pretty and tastes delicious!' Primrose, as well as being descriptive, is the Rosebery family name.

Serve on hot buttered toast.

# SMOKED SALMON
# AND GRAVAD LAX

Smoked salmon is one of those wonderful foods that is always welcome and almost impossible to tire of. At a party it is the smoked salmon canapés that disappear first and smoked salmon served with brown bread and butter and a slice of lemon is one of the easiest, but also one of the most appreciated of first courses.

Making your own gravad lax is easy, but smoking your own salmon is not something to do in the home as it requires some sort of smokery as well as a supply of oak chippings, and there is, as it says in the complicated instructions a friend sent me, the problem of trial and particularly of error!

It is easiest to buy smoked salmon already sliced and there are still some delicatessens who will slice it to order. Most shops now sell ready sliced packets and these come in all sizes from two slices to a beautifully presented whole side weighing around 1kg/2lb. The salmon is hand cut and the slices interleaved for ease of serving.

If you have the confidence to slice it yourself it is considerably cheaper to buy an uncut side, and salmon knives with a long blade and a fluted edge are available. Lay the side flat on a board; start slicing at the tail end and to obtain thin and reasonable sized slices keep the knife flat against the fish.

Offcuts or pieces from a side of smoked salmon can also sometimes be bought. They are cheap and need picking over to eliminate the tough bits and the brown fatty edges, but they are often worthwhile. In the recipes that follow pieces can be used whenever the salmon is cut into strips or chopped, but remember that there is a lot of wastage and that you will need to start with a larger quantity than that given in the list of ingredients.

There is a great difference in the smokes: some are very mild, others much more robust and sometimes tasting strongly of oak. Fish from any particular shop or smokery is usually fairly consistent, so if you find a smoke you really like, stick with it.

## Simple Smoked Salmon

If you are serving smoked salmon for a first course, you will need from 50-75g/2-3oz per head, depending on how lavish you want to be.

Lay the slices out on individual plates and place a wedge of lemon on the side.

Serve with thin slices of brown bread spread with unsalted butter, or with little cucumber sandwiches.

Pass the pepper grinder and some cayenne pepper round the table.

## Smoked Salmon Canapés

I give the simplest form of the ever useful smoked salmon canapé, but if you have time, or wish to push the boat out, you can glaze the salmon with a light jelly embedded with a tiny sprig of dill. You can also use biscuit cutters and turn out various shapes – Christmas trees make good seasonal party food.

Canapés are simple to make; butter slices of brown, wholemeal or rye bread and lay slices of smoked salmon on top. Squeeze on some lemon juice, grind on some pepper then cut off any crusts and cut each slice into squares or triangles.

You will need around 150g/5oz smoked salmon for every five slices of bread or every 20 canapés.

If you prefer to serve little rolls or Catherine wheels, spread large slices of bread with butter, lay on the salmon, sprinkle with lemon juice and pepper and then roll up. Wrap the rolls in foil and refrigerate until needed – this keeps them from unwinding. Finally, just before serving, cut each roll into half a dozen or so Catherine wheels.

## Asparagus and smoked salmon rolls

Cut the woody bottom from some thick asparagus spears and cook until tender. Butter some slices of brown bread, cut off the crusts, and lay a slice of smoked salmon on each. Put an asparagus spear on the top and roll into cigars.

# Fillings for Slices of Smoked Salmon: Rolls, Moulds, Terrines

Smoked salmon combines well with many other flavours and textures and slices can be rolled round a filling, or – and this is simpler – used to line ramekins, jam tart tins or one larger dish or bowl. Oil the dishes or tins so that you can turn out the finished moulds easily.

If you use individual ramekins you will need 175g/6oz smoked salmon to line four, but you may find that 125g/4oz is enough to line one larger dish or four jam tart tins.

## *Prawn and Apple*

125g/4oz PRAWNS, DEFROSTED
1 SMALL DESSERT APPLE
4 tbsp MAYONNAISE
1 tsp TOMATO PURÉE
SALT AND PEPPER

Peel the apple, cut the flesh into cubes and mix it with all the other ingredients.

## *Hardboiled Egg and Cress*

2 HARDBOILED EGGS, CHOPPED
PUNNET MUSTARD AND CRESS
2 tbsp MAYONNAISE
1 tbsp SINGLE CREAM OR FROMAGE FRAIS
PEPPER

Mix together the mayonnaise and cream or fromage frais, stir in the egg and mustard and cress and grind in some pepper.

# Beansprouts and Soy Sauce

Smoked salmon is surprisingly good with crunchy beansprouts, and this filling is not too rich.

250g/8oz BEANSPROUTS
2 tbsp SUNFLOWER OR VEGETABLE OIL
2 tsp SOY SAUCE
1 tbsp LEMON JUICE
PEPPER

Soak the beansprouts in cold water for 10 minutes then drain them. Bring a pan of water to the boil and blanch the beansprouts: plunge them into the water and leave for 1 minute. Drain them well, then roughly chop them.

In a bowl combine the oil, soy sauce and lemon juice and grind in some pepper. Add the beansprouts and toss them well.

# Smoked Trout and Almonds

Smoked trout is always a great favourite and I give two versions; the first with flaked fish and almonds is very quick to make, and the second is slightly more complicated with the smoked trout used to make a light mousse.

125g/4oz SMOKED TROUT, FLAKED
50g/1oz FLAKED ALMONDS
150ml/¼ pint DOUBLE CREAM
½-1 tsp HORSERADISH SAUCE
SQUEEZE LEMON JUICE
PINCH CAYENNE
SALT AND PEPPER

Brown the almonds under the grill. Lightly whip the cream, then mix in some horse-radish, lemon juice, cayenne and seasonings. Stir in the fish and the almonds, then taste and, if necessary, add more of the flavourings.

# Smoked Trout Mousse

This filling is very rich and this amount is adequate for six.

125g/4oz SMOKED TROUT
1 tbsp BUTTER
1 tbsp FLOUR
150ml/¼ pint MILK
1½ tsp GELATINE
1½ tsp BRANDY
LEMON JUICE
SALT AND PEPPER
150ml/¼ pint DOUBLE CREAM

Make a béchamel sauce with the butter, flour and milk, then turn it into a blender or food processor. Add the smoked trout and process until smooth. Melt the gelatine in 2 tbsp water and add it together with the brandy, a squeeze of lemon juice and some salt and pepper to the trout mixture. Process them in, check the seasoning and leave until it is about to set.

Lightly whip the cream and fold it into the trout mixture. Spoon into the prepared ramekins and fold over any overlapping pieces of smoked salmon. Cover each one with a piece of foil and refrigerate until needed.

To serve, place a little mixed greenery on each plate and turn the moulds out on to it. Garnish with a twist of lemon.

# Scrambled Eggs with Smoked Salmon

An evening watching television and eating scrambled eggs mixed with smoked salmon is my idea of perfect relaxation.

Roughly chop the smoked salmon, mix it with 2-3 tbsp double cream, grind in some pepper and leave to soak for 20-30 minutes.

Start making the scrambled eggs in the usual way and, when half cooked, stir in the salmon and cream.

## Ricotta and Fresh Herbs

Ricotta must be the freshest tasting of all dairy products and, although in Italy it is often used in sweet dishes, I find it makes a lovely foil for savoury flavours. Here, the ricotta is mixed with chives and parsley: try to buy the flat leaved variety, use lots of both so that they give a good crunch to the finished stuffing.

250g/8oz RICOTTA
5-6tbsp CHOPPED PARSLEY
2-3tbsp SNIPPED CHIVES
SALT AND PEPPER
EXTRA PARSLEY AND CHIVES FOR DECORATION

Mash the ricotta with a fork, adding the herbs and seasoning as you go along. Check how salty your smoked salmon is and adjust the salt accordingly.

Serve the moulds decorated with a few whole parsley leaves and some chives.

## Crab and Cucumber

The mixed textures of smoked salmon, crab meat and cucumber make an interesting combination.

This is best made with fresh crab meat, but good quality tins of white crab meat make an acceptable alternative.

125g/4oz WHITE CRAB MEAT
7.5-10cm/3-4 inches CUCUMBER, PEELED AND DICED
3 tbsp MAYONNAISE
1 tsp TOMATO PURÉE
PINCH CAYENNE (OPTIONAL)

Peel the cucumber, split it lengthwise, discard the seeds, then cut it into dice.

Mix the mayonnaise with the tomato purée and, if liked, a pinch of cayenne. Mix the crab meat and cucumber into the mayonnaise and use to fill the prepared ramekins.

Serve with a little lightly dressed tomato salad.

# Oeufs en Cocotte with Smoked Salmon

Oeufs en cocotte are very easy but they do need fairly careful timing as they are best eaten when the yolks are runny and the whites just set.

50g/2oz SMOKED SALMON, CHOPPED
4 tbsp SINGLE CREAM
SALT AND PEPPER
25g/1oz BUTTER
4 EGGS

Put the cream in a small bowl, stir in the smoked salmon and a generous grinding of pepper.

Generously butter four ramekins, break an egg into each one and lightly sprinkle with salt and pepper. Cover each ramekin with a piece of foil and put them in a shallow pan. Pour in boiling water to come halfway up the sides of the ramekins and put the pan in the oven.

Cook for 5 minutes, then remove from the oven and spoon the salmon and cream mixture on top of the eggs. Return to the oven for a further 7 minutes.

# Soufflé Omelette

For an easy omelette filling, soak the smoked salmon in cream, as given for the scrambled eggs, and add some chopped parsley or dill.

This is slightly more complicated, but the resulting omelette is wonderfully fluffy and light. These instructions are for an omelette for two people made in a medium sized, preferably nonstick frying pan, but if you have a large frying pan with a diameter of at least 32cm/12 inches, you can make a sensational looking omelette for four; all you need to do is double the ingredients and cook it for slightly longer. *Serves 2.*

75g/3oz SMOKED SALMON, CHOPPED
75ml/3fl oz SINGLE CREAM
3 EGGS
SALT AND PEPPER
25g/1oz BUTTER

Put the smoked salmon to soak in the cream and leave for half an hour or so.

Preheat the oven to 190°C/375°F/gas 5.

Separate the eggs. Season the yolks with pepper and a little salt and stir 2 tbsp of the cream into them. Whisk the whites until stiff and fold them into the yolk mixture.

Melt the butter in the frying pan and when it is hot pour in the egg mixture. Leave on the heat for 1-2 minutes for the bottom to set, then put the frying pan into the oven and leave for 3 minutes.

Remove from the oven and check that the omelette is cooked; it should have risen but still be soft in the centre. Spoon the salmon and remaining cream on to the omelette, fold it in half and slide in on to a serving dish. Eat immediately.

# Oeufs Pochés Bénédictine

A classic oeufs Bénédictine is made with slices of ham, but smoked salmon is just as good – no, I'm wrong – even better! It is a wonderfully rich dish for moments of self-indulgence. The variation with quails eggs makes a lovely party dish.

People seem to flap about poaching eggs, but provided the eggs are very fresh, it isn't difficult, and they can, as I suggest in the instructions, be made ahead.

The recipe for Hollandaise on page 44 makes a very generous amount for four people and it could easily be stretched to feed six. If you wish you could cut it by using 2 egg yolks and 125g/4oz butter.

4 EGGS

2 MUFFINS

4 SLICES SMOKED SALMON

HOLLANDAISE SAUCE (SEE PAGE 44)

Bring a pan of water to simmering point and carefully break 2 eggs into it. Keep the water at a gentle simmer and cook them for 2 minutes or until the white is opaque. Using a fish slice, gently lift out the eggs and drain on a clean kitchen towel. Cook the other 2 eggs in the same way. When the eggs are cool trim off any ragged edges and put them in a bowl of cold water in the fridge. They will keep for several hours.

When you are nearly ready to eat, make the Hollandaise sauce, then leave it for 5 minutes while you prepare the rest of the dish.

Split the muffins, lightly toast them and put to keep warm in a low oven. Take the eggs from the fridge and put them into a pan of simmering water for 1 minute.

Take the muffins from the oven and cover each half with a generous slice of smoked salmon. Take the eggs from the water, drain them and place on top of the salmon. Spoon the sauce over the top and serve immediately.

# Quails eggs Bénédictine

Make three or four for each person.

Poach the quails eggs following the instructions above, but cook them for only 45 seconds. Keep them in the fridge in a bowl of cold water.

Make a Hollandaise sauce: I like to use a yellow saffron flavoured one for this dish (see page 46).

Cut out small rounds of bread, fry them in butter, cover each one with a piece of smoked salmon of about the same size and place them on individual plates.

Bring the water back to the boil, quickly reheat the eggs, drain them well and place on top of the smoked salmon. Spoon some sauce over each one and serve.

# Filo Triangles

As well as being delicious on their own, scrambled eggs and smoked salmon make a good filling for little filo parcels. Serve them with drinks or as a first course. A plate with three triangles and a lightly dressed green garnish, of perhaps frisée and rocket, looks good and needs little last minute attention.

75g/3oz SMOKED SALMON
2 tbsp DOUBLE CREAM
25g/1oz BUTTER
2 EGGS
SALT AND PEPPER
CAYENNE PEPPER
ABOUT 250g/8oz FILO PASTRY
MELTED BUTTER

Roughly chop the smoked salmon and mix with the cream. Leave to soak for about half an hour.

Melt the butter in a small pan, break in the eggs and scramble over a low heat. When the eggs are nearly cooked, fold in the smoked salmon and cream and remove from the heat. Season with pepper, if needed, some salt and, if liked, some cayenne.

Melt some butter, unfold the filo sheets and keep them covered with a damp cloth. One sheet at a time, spread out the filo on your work surface and cut into strips of around 8-10cm/3½-4 inches wide. Brush each strip with melted butter and place a spoonful of filling about 2cm/¾ inch from the bottom. Fold a corner across to make a triangle and continue, folding in triangles, up the strip of pastry: there may well be an illustration showing how to do this on the instructions that come with the pastry. Place the finished triangle on a baking sheet and continue making pastry triangles until all the filling has been used up. Brush the top of the triangles with butter, cover with a damp cloth and leave until needed.

Heat the oven to 180°C/350°F/gas 4 and bake for 10-12 minutes or until golden and crisp. Serve while hot.

# Crêpes with Dill and Smoked Salmon

I have always liked pancakes and this makes a good lunch dish for four or a starter for eight. The pancake mixture makes enough for about 16 × 15cm/6 inch thin and lacey crêpes.

You can make the pancakes ahead, wrap them in foil and reheat for 30 minutes or so in a low oven, but neither the smoked salmon nor the soured cream should be cooked so, once filled, they should be eaten.

125g/4oz PLAIN FLOUR
½ tsp SALT
2 EGGS
300ml/½ pint MILK
2 tbsp CHOPPED DILL
BUTTER FOR FRYING

*For the filling*
250ml/8fl oz SOURED CREAM
250-300g/8-10oz SMOKED SALMON
PEPPER

Mix together the flour, salt and eggs, gradually beat in the milk and finally stir in the dill. Leave to stand for 30 minutes.

Heat a little butter in a small omelette or frying pan and pour in just enough mixture to cover the bottom. When the bottom is cooked, turn the pancake and cook the other side. Put the cooked pancakes on to a plate, interleave them with pieces of greaseproof paper and keep them warm in a low oven.

Grind some pepper into the soured cream and mix it in. Cut the smoked salmon into the required number of pieces. Just before serving, spread each crêpe with a little cream and put a slice of smoked salmon on the top. Fold the pancakes into quarters and serve immediately.

# Sushi Tart

This is an adaptation of sushi, that decorative Japanese dish of stuffed seaweed rolls. You need a special bamboo mat to roll up the sushi, so here I have put the vinegered rice between smoked salmon slices and then weighted it down.

The authentic ingredients are much the best and there are now many oriental stores that sell them. However, substitutes such as pudding rice, diluted white wine vinegar and English mustard are possible. *Serves 8-10 as a first course.*

*For the vinegared rice*
375g/12oz JAPANESE SUSHI RICE
4 tbsp RICE VINEGAR
1 tbsp WHITE SUGAR
1 tsp SALT

About an hour before cooking the rice, wash it, swirling it round with your hand, in several changes of water. When the water runs clear, pour the rice into a sieve and leave to drain, shaking occasionally, for 20 minutes or until it is dry.

Put the rice into a pan with a close fitting lid, pour in 450ml/¾ pint water and leave to soak for half an hour. Cover the pan and bring to the boil over a very high heat. Reduce the heat, simmer for 10 minutes, then turn the heat off and leave the pan to steam for a further 15 minutes. Do not at any stage remove the lid.

Warm the vinegar, stir in the sugar and salt, and when the sugar has melted, take from the heat and leave until needed.

Transfer the rice to a large bowl and sprinkle on the vinegar. Using a large wooden spoon, toss it until cool. In Japan the rice is fanned at the same time to make it glisten.

Use the prepared rice immediately or keep, for no more than 3 hours, covered with a damp cloth.

*For the tart*
125-175g/4-6oz SMOKED SALMON
1 tsp WASABI POWDER (JAPANESE HORSERADISH)
LEMON JUICE
THE PREPARED SUSHI RICE
1 tbsp JAPANESE SESAME SALT
1 tbsp CHOPPED DILL
JAPANESE SOY SAUCE

Line a 15-20cm/6-8 inch quiche tin or a dish with foil. Mix the wasabi powder with a teaspoon of water.

Sprinkle a little lemon juice over the foil, cover the bottom of the dish with half the smoked salmon, then brush it thinly with the wasabi paste.

Wet your hands and put the prepared rice into the tin. Spread it evenly and press it down hard, then cover it with the remaining smoked salmon. Sprinkle on a little more lemon juice and spread on some more wasabi. Cover with another piece of foil, then a plate or something similar. Weigh the plate down with weights or tins and leave for 2-3 hours.

Mix together the sesame salt and dill.

Just before serving, turn out the tart and peel off the foil. Using a small spatula or a teaspoon, press the dill and sesame salt to the outside rim of the tart. Cut it into thin slices with a wet knife and serve with soy sauce.

# Smoked Salmon Pâté

In Greece mashed potato is often used to give bulk to taramasalata. It works just as well with chopped smoked salmon and makes a pâté or dip that is both tasty and not too rich.

Don't try making this in a food processor, as the potatoes will become heavy and gluey.

175g/6oz SMOKED SALMON, FINELY CHOPPED
250g/8oz FLOURY POTATOES
1 SMALL SHALLOT, FINELY CHOPPED
2 tbsp SUNFLOWER OIL
ZEST OF 1 LEMON
SALT AND PEPPER

Boil the potatoes in salted water, then peel and mash them. Cook the shallot in the oil until soft.

Stir together the potatoes, shallot, salmon and lemon zest, add a good grinding of pepper and, if necessary, some salt.

Serve chilled with melba toast or hot pitta bread.

# Tagliatelle with Smoked Salmon

The Italians love smoked salmon, and this delicious combination is Italian rather than British in origin.

375g/12oz SMOKED SALMON, ROUGHLY CHOPPED
375g/12oz TAGLIATELLE
300ml/½ pint SINGLE CREAM
1 tbsp BRANDY
50g/2oz BUTTER
ZEST OF 1 LEMON
PEPPER

Put the cream, brandy, butter, lemon zest and a good grinding of black pepper into a large bowl and put it to heat in a low oven at 120°C/250°F/gas ½.

Cook the tagliatelle in a large pan of salted water, drain it, but not too well or it will stick together. Add the tagliatelle and the salmon to the warmed cream, toss gently and serve at once.

# Citrus Fruit, Avocado and Smoked Salmon Salad

This always looks and tastes very fresh.

4 SLICES SMOKED SALMON
1 AVOCADO PEAR
JUICE OF 1 LIME
2 ORANGES OR A PINK GRAPEFRUIT
4 tbsp OLIVE OR SUNFLOWER OIL
PINCH SUGAR
SALT AND PEPPER

Put a slice of smoked salmon on to each of four plates.

Cut the avocado into quarters, peel and slice them and arrange each quarter in a fan on the plates. Brush them with a little of the lime juice.

Peel the oranges or grapefruit, remove all the pith and skin and cut out the separate segments. Add them to the arrangement on the plates.

Make a vinaigrette with the oil and remaining lime juice and season to taste with sugar, salt and pepper. Spoon it over the plates.

Papaya, wild rice and smoked salmon

# Pasta and Smoked Salmon Salad

This salad is good and easy summer lunch or buffet food.

300g/10oz SMOKED SALMON, ROUGHLY CHOPPED
300g/10oz SMALL MACARONI OR SIMILAR PASTA
1 tbsp OLIVE OIL
125ml/4fl oz MAYONNAISE
1 tbsp CHOPPED DILL
JUICE AND ZEST OF ½ LEMON
PEPPER

Cook the pasta, drain it and rinse under cold running water. Toss it with the oil and leave until needed.

Mix the smoked salmon into the mayonnaise with the dill, lemon juice and zest. Just before serving stir in the pasta and grind over some pepper.

# Salad of Flageolet Beans with Smoked Salmon

It may be cheating to use canned beans, but it's quick. If you have the time, soak and cook the flageolets or some green lentils, for a more authentic taste. *As a first course serves 4-6.*

400g/14oz CAN FLAGEOLET BEANS
2 LEMONS
4 tbsp OLIVE OIL
1-2 SHALLOTS, FINELY CHOPPED
SALT AND PEPPER
75-125g/3-4oz SMOKED SALMON
MIXED GREEN LEAVES

Drain and thoroughly rinse the beans. Grate the rind of one lemon and squeeze out the juice.

In a bowl mix together the olive oil, 2 tbsp lemon juice, the lemon zest and the shallot. Stir in the beans, season with salt and pepper and leave until needed.

Arrange a nest of salad leaves on four or six plates. Cut the smoked salmon into strips and stir it into the beans. Spoon the bean mixture into the centre of the plates and garnish with the second lemon, cut into wedges.

Gravad lax with mustard sauce

# Papaya, Wild Rice and Smoked Salmon

This is a lovely combination of flavours and colours and is especially good in the winter when our native fruits are in short supply.

50g/2oz WILD RICE
125g/4oz SMOKED SALMON
1 tbsp WHITE WINE VINEGAR
3 tbsp SUNFLOWER OIL
SALT AND PEPPER
2 PAPAYAS
1 LIME

Wash the wild rice, then cook it in salted water for around 40 minutes or until tender. Drain and turn into a bowl.

Cut the smoked salmon into strips and mix them into the wild rice.

Make a dressing with the vinegar and oil, season it well with salt and pepper and mix it into the rice and salmon.

When you are nearly ready to eat, cut the papayas in half and spoon out and discard all the black seeds. Cut the lime in half, squeeze a little juice over each piece of papaya and then spoon the wild rice mixture into the cavities. Cut the remaining half lime into four and use as a garnish.

# Quiche with Smoked Salmon and Courgettes

In common with all quiches, this is a good standby and is suitable for lunch, picnics or supper. It can be made with the cheaper smoked salmon pieces, but trim them carefully and cut out any dark or dry bits.

Small sweet tasting courgettes are best; if you can only find the larger ones you may need to get rid of the bitter juices by salting and draining before adding them to the custard mixture.

In the winter the courgettes can be replaced by Jerusalem artichokes. Peel them, cut them into even chunks, steam or boil for a few minutes and then use as given for the courgettes.

The pastry is best made in a food processor, as the almonds need to be finely chopped before being mixed with the flour. Although ground almonds can be used, they are too fine, and a lot of the pleasant crunch of this pastry is lost. If you are going to make the pastry case ahead you may find that it develops cracks as it cools: one way to stop too many large holes appearing is to paint over the bottom with some white of egg 5 minutes before it has finished cooking. Return the pastry to the oven and the egg should set to form a film over the base.

*For the pastry*
50g/2oz ALMONDS
175g/6oz PLAIN FLOUR
SALT AND CAYENNE PEPPER
125g/4oz BUTTER, CUBED
1 EGG YOLK

Put the almonds in a food processor and process until they are fairly finely chopped. Add the flour, a pinch of salt and a pinch of cayenne, and process for a few seconds to mix. Add the butter, and process until you reach the breadcrumb stage. Lightly beat the egg yolk with a scant tablespoon of cold water and then dribble it into the bowl. Process again, and stop the moment the pastry forms a ball. If it doesn't do so, you may need to add a little more water.

Chill the pastry well, then roll out and line a 23-25cm/9-10 inch flan tin. The pastry may be crumbly, but as it is made with an egg yolk you can patch up the sides with any extra bits. Chill again before baking. Heat the oven to 200°C/400°F/gas 6. Line the flan with foil, and bake for 15 minutes. Remove the foil, lower the oven to 150°C/300°F/gas 2, and bake for a further 10 minutes, or until the pastry is golden and cooked.

*For the filling*
50g-125g/2-4oz SMOKED SALMON, DEPENDING ON YOUR GENEROSITY
125g/4oz COURGETTES, SLICED
2 EGGS
1 EGG YOLK
300ml/½ pint SINGLE CREAM, OR A MIXTURE OF CREAM AND CRÈME FRAÎCHE
SALT AND PEPPER

Cut the smoked salmon into strips. Preheat the oven to 160°C/325°F/gas 3.

Mix together the eggs, egg yolk, and cream, and add the smoked salmon and courgettes. Season, remembering the smoked salmon may be salty, and stir together lightly.

Pour the mixture into the prepared case and bake for 25 minutes, or until the custard has set. If it starts to brown too much, cover it with a piece of foil. It is best served while still warm.

# Roli-Poli Pignoli
# (Pinenut Roulade)

This roulade was both thought up and named by my daughter and it makes a scrumptious first course for six to eight.

125g/4oz PINENUTS
50g/2oz FRESH BREADCRUMBS
SALT AND PEPPER
4 EGGS, SEPARATED
375g/12oz ASPARAGUS
125g/4oz SMOKED SALMON
HOLLANDAISE SAUCE MADE WITH 4 EGGS AND 250g/8oz BUTTER, SEE PAGE 44

Line a Swiss roll tin of approximately 33 × 23cm/13 × 9 inches with silicone or greased greaseproof paper and preheat the oven to 190°C/375°F/gas 5.

Chop the pinenuts in a food processor or crush them with a rolling pin. Mix them with the breadcrumbs, season with salt and pepper and stir in the egg yolks. Add a pinch of salt to the egg whites and whisk until stiff. Stir a spoonful of the egg whites into the pinenut mixture, lightly fold in the rest, then spoon it into the prepared tin. Bake for about 8 minutes or until the centre is springy to the touch and the whole is lightly browned.

Meanwhile, cut any woody ends from the asparagus, and steam or boil until tender. Make the Hollandaise sauce.

Spread a damp tea towel on the work surface, cover it with a sheet of greaseproof paper and turn the cooked roulade on to it. Spread the roulade with about a third of the Hollandaise, cover with the smoked salmon, and arrange the asparagus on top. Roll it up using the greaseproof paper.

You can either eat it immediately, or you can wrap it in foil and warm it quickly in a hot oven at the last minute. Serve it in slices, with an extra spoonful of Hollandaise on the side of the plate.

# Risotto with Lemon and Smoked Salmon

Risotto, like hot soup, is both comforting and reviving. Its only drawback is that it has to be made at the last minute, but it is not too exacting, and sitting by the cooker and stirring, especially if a bottle of wine has been opened and friends are present, can also be comforting.

250g/8oz SMOKED SALMON TRIMMINGS
5 tbsp DOUBLE CREAM
900ml/1½ pints LIGHTLY SALTED CHICKEN OR VEGETABLE STOCK
50g/2oz UNSALTED BUTTER
1 tbsp SUNFLOWER OIL
2 SHALLOTS, FINELY CHOPPED
375g/12oz ARBORIO OR RISOTTO RICE
150ml/¼ pint DRY WHITE WINE
ZEST AND JUICE OF ½ LEMON
2-3 LEAVES SAGE, FINELY CHOPPED
3 tbsp GRATED PARMESAN CHEESE
SALT AND PEPPER

Trim the smoked salmon of any brown or fatty bits, cut it into bite size pieces and in a bowl mix into the cream. Heat the stock and keep it at a gentle simmer.

In a heavy based saucepan heat half the butter and the oil. Add the shallots and cook until they soft. Stir in the rice. When it is shiny and translucent, pour in the wine, and stir in the lemon zest and sage. Cook, still stirring, until most of the liquid has disappeared, then add the hot stock a ladle at a time. Keep the rice at a gentle bubble, and wait until each ladleful has been almost all absorbed before adding the next. Continue until the rice is soft but not mushy. You may not need to use all the stock or you may, at the end, have to add a little hot water.

Take the pan from the heat, stir in the remaining butter, the lemon juice, grated Parmesan and lots of freshly ground black pepper. Finally add the smoked salmon and cream, stir it in, check if further salt is needed, and serve immediately.

# Gravad Lax

Gravad lax is Scandinavia's answer to Scotland's smoked salmon. Its origins may well be older, but both methods of preserving were invented to keep salmon through long dark northern winters. Gravad lax was originally made by wrapping the fish in a birch twig parcel and burying it in the ground under a weight. It was unearthed and eaten after a few days, when it would have been similar to the gravad lax we know, but in the depths of winter the fish was left for several weeks, by which time the flesh had fermented.

Until recently, gravad lax was virtually unknown outside Scandinavia. One of the earliest mentions must be the one I came across in *Cooking with Bon Viveur*, which was published in 1955. The recipe starts: 'A strange and delicate treatment of salmon: this is Scandinavian and almost unbelievably good.' Then, after describing how to make gravad lax, it finishes: 'Slice thinly and serve with a heart-of-a-lettuce salad, dressed with pure grape juice from white muscatel grapes.' That could be very good.

Like smoked salmon, gravad lax is often served with brown bread and butter, but for finger eats, I prefer to use rye bread, or to serve it on lightly buttered slices of malt loaf. If I am serving gravad lax as a first course I accompany it with hot, boiled or steamed salad potatoes. I believe that gravad lax, potatoes and dill and mustard sauce are often served together in Scandinavia and I find they make a delicious trio.

When making gravad lax, the measurement of salt is important. Use too much and the result will be unpleasantly salty. Use too little and the juices will not be drawn out and the fish will be tough and remain 'raw'. If after a day there is still only a small amount of juice in your dish, you can sprinkle on a little more salt, but be prudent with the amount. Use lots of dill, which grows in profusion in Scandinavia and is the traditional flavouring for gravad lax.

You can make gravad lax using a whole salmon or, if that is too much, use the tail end, but 750g/1½lb fish from a 1-1.2kg/2¼-2½lb piece of tail is about the smallest practical amount. The fish needs to be filleted, but not skinned, and very carefully boned. The brandy is optional but it won't toughen the flesh and it adds a rich warm flavour.

For each 750g/1½lb salmon you will need:

1 tbsp BRANDY (OPTIONAL)
2 tbsp SALT
1 tbsp SUGAR
2 tsp PEPPER
LARGE BUNCH DILL

Clean the fish by wiping it with a piece of kitchen paper and sprinkle on the brandy if you are using it. Mix together the salt, sugar and pepper.

Use a shallow dish or a plate long enough to hold the salmon fillets. Lay a bed of dill in it, cover with a piece of the salmon, skin side down, and sprinkle on half the salt mixture. Add a thick layer of dill, then sprinkle on the remaining salt mixture and cover it with the second salmon fillet, skin side up. Put any remaining stems of dill on the top. Cover the plate or dish with a double layer of foil and place a board or something similar on the top. Weigh it down with weights or tins, using about the same weight as the salmon.

Put it in the bottom of the fridge. Turn the salmon and spoon the juices back into the centre every 12 hours. After 3 days cut off a sliver to taste and see if it is ready; if not, add a little more salt and leave for another 24 hours.

When it is ready dry the fish and remove any salt residue by patting with kitchen paper, then wrap in foil and refrigerate until needed. It will keep for 3-4 days.

To serve: remove it from the fridge, sprinkle with a little chopped dill and cut into thin slices, like smoked salmon. You could also skin it and leave it in fillets. Accompany it with the dill and mustard sauce given below.

# Dill and Mustard Sauce

3 tbsp DIJON MUSTARD
2 tbsp WHITE WINE VINEGAR
1 tbsp LIGHT SOFT BROWN SUGAR
150ml/¼ pint SUNFLOWER OR GRAPESEED OIL
SALT AND PEPPER
2 tbsp FINELY CHOPPED DILL

Mix together the mustard, vinegar and sugar, and then, as if making mayonnaise, gradually whisk in the oil. Add salt and pepper to taste and stir in the dill. The sauce will keep covered and refrigerated for a few days. If it separates, whisk to amalgamate before serving.

# Tarragon Gravad Lax

However good a basic dish, there comes a time when chefs start chopping and changing it and gravad lax has followed this path and stood up well to experiments. Try making it with another herb: tarragon is especially good, but remember to continue the theme and to flavour the sauce in the same way. The two variations below are more unusual, and also worth trying.

# Spiced Gravad Lax

This may sound weird, but in fact it is rather good. When I first started on this recipe I thought I might use a combination of some of the more unusual spices, but after spending ages going through my spice cupboard and every book I could find on the subject, I settled for something that was really simple. I tried it and everybody liked it.

The next hurdle was the sauce, and amazing experiments took place, but in the end I found it difficult to beat the traditional Scandinavian sweet mustard sauce, though a little coriander chopped into it is a good addition.

By this time my family and friends had formed a sort of 'spiced gravad lax committee', and our last resolution was that it should be served with black rye bread or pumpernickel – I hope you agree.

For each 750g/1½lb salmon you will need:

2 tbsp SEA SALT
1 tbsp SOFT BROWN SUGAR
1 tsp GROUND MIXED PEPPER: RED, GREEN AND BLACK
½ tsp GROUND CINNAMON
½ tsp GROUND CLOVES
½ tsp GROUND GINGER
½ tsp GRATED NUTMEG

Mix everything together, rub the mixture over the salmon and follow the directions in the main recipe on page 166.

To serve

Follow the directions for the Dill and mustard sauce on page 167, but replace the dill with 1 tbsp finely chopped coriander.

Cut the fish into thin slices and serve with rye bread and the sauce.

# Citrus Gravad Lax

Christian Fuentes gave me this idea and to illustrate how much zest to use, he held out the palm of one hand and drew a circle on it with the index finger of the other. I don't know if I have interpreted it as he meant it, but the result is good and the citrus flavours, being not too pronounced, blend into the salmon and seem to linger nicely on the palate.

The thyme flavoured sauce is sweetened with honey and, conveniently, can be made with the juice of the fruits. After removing the zest, wrap the fruits in foil, put them in the fridge, and they will keep for the two or three days that the salmon needs to marinate.

My addition to Christian's idea is to serve the gravad lax on a small nest of warm tagliatelle. The pasta, like the potatoes I suggest serving with the dill gravad lax, provides a good background to both the sauce and the fish and rounds off the dish very well.

For each 750g/1½ lb salmon you will need:

2 tbsp SEA SALT<br>
1 tbsp SUGAR<br>
ZEST OF 1 ORANGE, ½ LEMON, AND ½ LIME<br>
1 tbsp BRANDY (OPTIONAL)

Mix together the salt, sugar and zests, and make the gravad lax following the main recipe on page 166.

*For the thyme and honey sauce*<br>
1 EGG YOLK<br>
1 tsp DIJON MUSTARD<br>
SALT AND PEPPER<br>
JUICE FROM THE ORANGE, LEMON AND LIME<br>
150ml/¼ pint LIGHT OIL, SUNFLOWER OR GRAPESEED<br>
2 tbsp RUNNY HONEY<br>
1 tsp FINELY CHOPPED THYME, OR ½ tsp DRIED THYME<br>
A LITTLE FINELY GRATED ORANGE ZEST

Make as for a mayonnaise. Mix the egg yolk with the mustard, pepper, and 1 tbsp each lime and lemon juice, then slowly whisk in the oil. When all the oil has been incorporated, stir in the honey, the thyme and the orange zest and season with salt. Thin the mayonnaise by stirring in some orange juice and finally, after tasting, adjust the lemon/lime, honey and salt content.

*To serve*

For each person you will need around 50g/2oz tagliatelle and 40g/1½oz gravad lax. Cook the pasta, toss it in the sauce, divide it between individual plates and arrange the sliced gravad lax over the top.

169

# Preserved Gravad Lax

Gravad lax can be preserved in oil and kept refrigerated for 2-3 weeks. Follow the directions for making gravad lax, but marinate the fish for only 30-36 hours. Drain off the juices and wipe off the salt and dill with kitchen paper. Pack the salmon into a jar or a dish and cover it completely in sunflower oil. Seal the jar or cover the dish tightly with 2 layers of foil and keep refrigerated until needed.

You can make very attractive presents by slicing the marinated salmon and then packing the slices along with some freshly blanched dill into a glass jar. Fill the jar with oil and seal tightly.

I did try using olive oil, but found it rather heavy and preferred the salmon when preserved with sunflower oil. When you eat the salmon you can drain off the oil and use it in the same way again.

# RECIPES FROM CHEFS

Many of the Master Chefs of Great Britain buy and use superior quality Shetland salmon and I am very grateful to them for their generosity in passing on some recipes from their kitchens that are not too difficult to cook at home. At the end I have added a recipe from John Nicolson, my fishmonger in Chiswick.

## *Dressed Salmon*

From the Champany Inn, Linlithgow, near Edinburgh; Chef and Proprietor Clive Davidson.

Clive Davidson says that the marinade is enough for 2.3kg/5lb salmon, which would give fillets for 8 people.

8 PIECES OF FILLET

*For the marinade*
600ml/1 pint WATER
2 tbsp WHITE PEPPERCORNS
300g/10oz CASTER SUGAR
½ tsp MIXED SPICE
4 BAY LEAVES
1 LARGE SPANISH ONION, THINLY SLICED INTO RINGS

Put the marinade ingredients into a pan and boil for 1 minute.

Steam or poach the salmon fillets until tender, then skin them. Place the fillets in a deep dish and cover with the hot marinade. Allow to cool. Lift from the marinade before serving.

The salmon will keep in the marinade, well covered and refrigerated, for up to 3 days.

# Hot Salmon and Seafood Sausage on a little Stew of Mussels

From the Murrayshall Country House Hotel, Scone, Perthshire; Chef Bruce Sangster.

175g/6oz FRESH SALMON, BONED AND SKINNED
1 EGG WHITE
300ml/½ pint DOUBLE CREAM
SALT, PEPPER, NUTMEG
BUNCH OF DILL, CHOPPED
125g/4oz ASSORTED SEAFOOD, CUT INTO SMALL PIECES

*For the stew*
600ml/1 pint FRESH MUSSELS, CLEANED AND DE-BEARDED
150ml/¼ pint DRY VERMOUTH
150ml/¼ pint FISH STOCK
50g/2oz MIXED VEGETABLES: CARROT, ONION, LEEK, CELERY, FINELY DICED
150ml/¼ pint DOUBLE CREAM
2 TOMATOES, SKINNED, DESEEDED AND DICED
BUNCH CHIVES, CHOPPED
50g/2oz COLD BUTTER

Liquidize together the salmon and egg white, pass through a fine sieve and place in a bowl over ice to cool. Carefully mix in the double cream. Check the consistency (it should hold together) and season with salt, pepper and nutmeg. Finally mix in the dill and fold in the assorted seafood.

Pipe the mixture on to a sheet of clingfilm, then carefully roll up into one large sausage.

Divide into 4 equal sections and twist into links. Using pieces of string, tie between each sausage. Poach them slowly, in a large pan of simmering water, for 8-10 minutes.

Place the mussels and vermouth in a pan with a tightly fitting lid. Steam until the mussels open, then remove and shell them.

Strain the pan juices through muslin to remove any grit. Place the juices, the fish stock and vegetables in a clean pan, and cook for 2-3 minutes. Add the double cream and cook until the sauce is of a coating consistency.

Add the mussels to the sauce, reheat, then add the tomato dice and chopped chives. Finish by stirring in knobs of cold butter.

Remove the clingfilm from the sausages and serve with the mussel stew.

# Salmon Kebabs

From the Ardanaiseig Hotel, Kilchrenan, near Taynult, Argyllshire; Chef, Lindsay Little.

16 × 2.5cm/1 inch CUBES SALMON
16 DRIED APRICOTS
1 GREEN PEPPER, DICED
8 SHALLOTS, HALVED

*For the marinade*
6 tbsp OLIVE OIL
1 tsp CHOPPED PARSLEY
1 tsp CHOPPED CHERVIL
1 tsp CHOPPED DILL
ZEST OF 1 LEMON

Mix all the marinade ingredients together well.

Assemble the kebabs on 4 skewers, dividing everything equally. Place in the marinade, ensuring the salmon is covered. Turn every 30 minutes for 4 hours.

When marinading is completed, place the skewers on a hot frying pan or barbecue. Lightly cook on all sides.

Serve with a crisp salad and new potatoes.

# Fillet of Salmon in Filo Pastry

From the Painswick Hotel, Painswick, Gloucestershire; Chef, Somerset Moore.

For each person take a 150g/5oz piece of salmon fillet, season well and place on a piece of filo pastry over twice the size of the fish. Place a julienne of carrots and leeks on top of the fish. Seal the parcel with melted butter and cook in preheated oven, at 180°C/350°F/ gas 4 for 15 minutes.

Meanwhile, make a chive and butter sauce. Reduce some white wine and fish stock to approximately half, and add the same amount of double cream. Whisk in small lumps of cold butter until the sauce thickens and stir in some chopped chives.

Serve the salmon parcels with the sauce.

# Escalopes of Salmon with Fresh Herbs

From the Old Beams Restaurant, Leek Road, Waterhouses, Staffordshire; Chef, Nigel Wallis.

4 × 175-250g/6-8oz SALMON ESCALOPES, BONED AND SKINNED
A FEW SPRIGS OF CHERVIL, TARRAGON AND BASIL, CHOPPED
SALT AND PEPPER
1 GLASS CHARDONNNAY
60g/2½oz COLD BUTTER, DICED

Grease an ovenproof dish big enough to hold the escalopes in one layer and lay them in it. Sprinkle half the herbs over the salmon. Season and pour on the wine. Cover with foil and prick the top to allow the steam to escape.

Heat gently on top of the stove for 15-20 seconds, then transfer immediately to a medium hot oven (180°C/350°F/gas 4) for approximately 4 minutes. The fish should remain moist and succulent.

Remove the dish from the oven, remove the foil and place the salmon on hot plates.

Pour the liquor into a shallow pan and boil rapidly until reduced by half (about 1 minute). Whisk in the butter. When thoroughly mixed, remove from the heat, add the remaining chopped herbs and pour over the salmon to serve.

# Salmon and Sole Pillows

From John Nicolson, Fishmonger, Devonshire Road, Chiswick, London W4.

2 LARGE LEMON SOLES
1 LARGE TAIL END CUTLET OF SALMON
4 SMALL OR 2 LARGE SCALLOPS
4 LARGE UNCOOKED KING PRAWN TAILS
PARSLEY TO GARNISH

Ask your fishmonger to fillet and skin the lemon soles, taking care to trim off the untidy 'frill' on each fillet, and also to fillet and skin the salmon cutlet, and divide this into 4 equal pieces.

Place the sole fillets skin side down on your work surface. Place a whole small scallop in the centre (or half a large scallop) and put a piece of salmon on top of the scallop. Now fold the top and tail of the fillet over the salmon and secure the whole thing by pushing a cocktail stick right through from top to bottom.

Turn the parcel upside down and push the stick through so that most of it protrudes from the top of the pillow. Impale a peeled, uncooked king prawn tail on each stick and then bake the lot, completely sealed in foil, for 20 minutes, at 180°C/350°F/gas 4.

Serve with a watercress or saffron sauce (page 62 or page 46).

# Fillet of Salmon with a Brioche Herb Crust

From Redmond's at Malvern View, Bishops Cleeve Hill, Gloucestershire; Chef and Proprietor, Redmond Hayward.

*Serves 2*
2 × 150g/5oz SALMON FILLETS
PARSLEY, BASIL, CHIVES, ROSEMARY
75g/3oz FINE BRIOCHE CRUMBS
SALT AND PEPPER
OLIVE OIL

Mix the finely chopped herbs with the brioche crumbs in a food processor. Season and pour a little olive oil into the mixture. Divide between the two fillets of salmon, place on a greased tray and cook at 190°C/375°F/gas 5 for approximately 5 minutes.

Serve with the sauce, below.

# Leek and Lemon Butter Sauce

2 SHALLOTS, FINELY CHOPPED
250g/8oz UNSALTED BUTTER
125ml/4fl oz DRY WHITE WINE
JUICE OF 1 LEMON
50g/2oz BLANCHED LEEK, FINELY CHOPPED

Sweat the shallots, without colouring, in 50g/2oz of the butter for 1-2 minutes. Add the white wine and boil until the liquid has reduced by half.

Take the pan off the heat and whisk in a further 50g/2oz butter. Return to a low heat and whisk in the remaining butter, 50g/2oz at a time. Add the lemon juice.

Garnish with finely chopped leek.

# Bibliography

ANDOH, ELIZABETH, *An American Taste of Japan*; William Morrow, 1985

ARIS, PEPITA, *The Sauce Book*; Century, 1984

AVILA, KAY, *Take Six More Cooks*; Thames Macdonald, 1988

BISSELL, FRANCES, *Oriental Flavours*; Pavilion, 1990

BON VIVEUR, *Cooking with Bon Viveur*; Museum Press, 1955

BRENNAN, JENNIFER, *The Cuisines of Asia*; Macdonald, 1984

CASAS, PENELOPE, *Tapas*; Pavilion, 1987

COSTA, MARGARET, *Four Seasons Cookery Book*; Thomas Nelson, 1970

DAVENPORT, PHILIPPA, *Cooking for Family and Friends*; Jill Norman & Hobhouse, 1982

DAVID, ELIZABETH, *French Provincial Cooking*; Michael Joseph, 1960

DAVIDSON, ALAN, *North Atlantic Seafood*; Macmillan, 1979

DOWNER, LESLEY & YONEDA, MINORU, *Step-by-Step Japanese Cooking*; Macdonald, 1985

'FRANCINE', *Vogue's French Cookery Book*; Condé Naste, 1961

GORDON, VICTOR, *Prawnography*; Bloomsbury, 1989

GRIGSON, JANE, *English Food*; 1974. *Fish Cookery*; IWFS, 1973. *Jane Grigson's Vegetable Book*; Michael Joseph, 1978. *The Observer Guide to British Cookery*; Michael Joseph, 1984

HANBURY TENISON, MARIKA, *Magimix Cookery*; ICTC 1982

HARBEN, PHILIP, *The Way to Cook*; The Bodley Head, 1945

HARRIS, VALENTINA, *Perfect Pasta*; Granada, 1984

HARTLEY, DOROTHY, *Food in England*; Macdonald, 1954

HICKS, SUSAN, *The Fish Course*; BBC 1987

HOLUIGUE, DIANE, *Master Class*; Simon & Schuster, 1988

HOM, KEN, *Ken Hom's Chinese Cookery*; BBC, 1984. *East Meets West Cuisine*; Macmillan, 1987

JAFFREY, MADHUR, *A Taste of India*; Pavilion, 1985

JUMP, MEG, *Cooking with Chillies*; The Bodley Head, 1989

KAFKA, BARBARA, *Microwave Gourmet*; Barrie & Jenkins, 1989

LEITH, PRUE & WALDEGRAVE, CAROLINE, *Leith's Cookery School*; Macdonald, 1985

LASSALLE, GEORGE, *Fish and Shellfish*; Sainsbury: Walker Books 1986

LOUSADA, PATRICIA, *Easy to Entertain*; Penguin, 1986

LUARD, ELISABETH, *European Peasant Cookery*; Bantam Press, 1986

NORMAN, JILL, *The Complete Book of Spices*; Dorling Kindersley 1990

OLNEY, RICHARD, *Simple French Food*; Jill Norman, 1974

RAFFAEL, MICHAEL, *Fresh from the Sea*; The Bodley Head, 1989

RODEN, CLAUDIA, *A New Book of Middle Eastern Food*; Viking, 1985

RUSHDIE, SAMEEN, *Sameen Rushdie's Indian Cookery*; Century, 1988

SEED, DIANE, *Favourite Indian Food*; Rosendale Press, 1990

SHAW, NANCY, *Food for the Greedy*; Cobden-Sanderson, 1936

SIMON, ANDRÉ L. *A Concise Encyclopedia of Gastronomy*, Allen Lane, 1952

SPRY, CONSTANCE & HUME, ROSEMARY, *The Constance Spry Cookery Book*; J.M. Dent, 1956

SO, YAN-KIT, *Wok Cookbook*; Piatkus, 1985

STEIN, RICHARD, *English Seafood Cookery*; Penguin, 1988

STYLE, SUE, *Creative Cookery*; Ebury Press, 1988

TIMS, BARBARA (ed), *Food in Vogue*; Pyramid, 1988

McANDREW, IAN, *A Feast of Fish*; Macdonald Orbis, 1987

McDOUALL, ROBIN, *Robin McDouall's Cookery Book*; Michael Joseph, 1963

OWEN, SRI, *Indonesian & Thai Cookery*; Piatkus, 1988

PERRY, KARIN, *The Fish Book*; Chatto & Windus 1989

TURNER, MRS ELSIE, *Fifty Ways of Cooking Fish*; 1933

WILLAN, ANNE, *Real Food*; Macmillan, 1988. *Reader's Digest Complete Guide to Cookery*; Dorling Kindersley, 1990.

WRIGHT, HANNAH, *Soups*; Robert Hale, 1985

WYSSENBACH, WILLY (ed), *Salmon*; Ebury Press, 1987. *Elle Cookbook*; Michael Joseph, 1981

# Useful addresses

Mail-order smoked salmon may be obtained from the following firms.

Shetland Smoked Salmon Co. Ltd
Browns Road
Lerwick
Shetland
ZE1 0ND

Contact: Eddie Barclay
Tel: 0595 5890
Fax: 0595 5139

The Shetland Smokehouse
Skeld
Shetland
ZE2 9NS

Contact: David Hammond
Tel: 0595 86251
Fax: 0595 86304

# INDEX